Radical Golf

Radical

Golf

How to Lower Your Score and
Raise Your Enjoyment of the Game

MICHAEL LAUGHLIN

Illustrations by Harry Trumbore

CROWN TRADE PAPERBACKS
New York

Published by Crown Trade Paperbacks, 201 East 50th Street, New York, New York 10022. Member of the Crown Publishing Group.

Random House, Inc. New York, Toronto, London, Sydney, Auckland

CROWN TRADE PAPERBACKS and colophon are trademarks of Crown Publishers, Inc.

Printed in the United States of America

Design by Susan Hood

Library of Congress Cataloging-in-Publication Data

Laughlin, Michael.
    Radical golf: how to lower your score and raise your enjoyment of the game/by Michael Laughlin; illustrations by Harry Trumbore.—1st ed.
    1. Golf—Study and teaching. I. Title.
GV962.5.K38 1996
796.352'07—dc20

ISBN 0-517-88626-X

10 9 8 7 6 5 4 3 2 1

First Edition

Dedicated to the memory of
Tony Phipps

Acknowledgments

I'm grateful to a really wonderful editor, Peter Ginna, and others who have take an interest or influenced me—sometimes inadvertently—in this project: George Surratt in Hawaii; my friend Howard Salen; Christina Robert; my agents, Witherspoon and Associates; Donald Laughlin; Fred Couples; our illustrator Harry Trumbore; and my colleague Pat McCarney.

Contents

Introduction   xiii

Part One: The Radical Philosophy   *1*

The Basic Principles of Radical Golf   3

How Not to Get Around a Golf Course   8

The Nub of the Big Secret Is Simple Mathematics   11

How to Keep Score   13

Follow Me Around Nine Holes   16

Putting and Lag Putting   19

Following the Four Champions Around   24

Finding Your Own "Free Throw"   27

What to Do When You're *Not* Playing Golf   30

Recapitulation; Where Are We So Far?   34

Part Two: How to Do It   **35**

The Great Leap Forward   37

Loving the Wedge   39

The Moment of Enlightenment   46

Portrait of a Thirty-five-Year-Old Radical Golfer   47

Let's Talk About Your Weapons   51

The Most Overlooked Aspect of the Game of Golf   54

The Medium Irons   57

The Long Irons   58

When to Play Short? When to Hit It!   60

Success, Failure, and Golf   61

Your Fiancé, Your Spouse, Your Marriage, and Golf   62

Golf Is Really Par-Three Golf!   63

The Big Challenge   64

Portrait of a Sixty-four-Year-Old Radical Golfer   65

A Bad Round of Golf   66

Riding the Escalator Down: Two Scorecards   68

How to Dress for Golf   72

Thinking Your Way Around the Course   77

The Radical Golfer vs. Tom Watson   79

A Review of the Match   85

Ranking the Shots   86

The Teenage Radical Golfer   88

Mapping the Course   90

How to Break Down a Course for Playing a Round   92

Your Home Course   115

The Hazards, the Out-of-Bounds, the Lakes, the Ponds   116

Part Three: Satisfactions   *119*

Should a Man Ever Play Golf with a Woman?   121

What Shots to Practice   124

Let's Review   126

The Radical Golfer's Hot Round   127

The Industrialization of Golf   129

The Golf Course Has to Be Sacrosanct   130

The Animal Kingdom   133

Where to Live or Spend Some Time If You Want to Play Some Golf   135

The Radical Golfer Goes to the Hawaiian Islands   137

The Radical Golfer Goes to Scotland and Ireland   140

The Relationship Between Golf and the Free Enterprise System   141

Always Play with a New Ball   142

Portrait of an Eighty-Year-Old Radical Golfer (My Dad)   144

Radical Golf Goes on Tour   147

Part Four: A Graduate Degree in Radical Golf   *149*

You Bought Your Woods, You Like Your Woods . . . When Can You Hit Them?   151

Once Again, the Trouble with Woods   152

The Absolute Most Important Shot   153

Do You Need to Take Lessons?   155
Across the Sand to a Tight Pin   156
Out of Sand to a Tight Pin   157
In a Fairway Bunker   158
The Knockdown   159
A Bad Start   161
Practice   162
Breaking 80   163
A Little Parable   164
Smoking on the Golf Course   167
Drinking on the Golf Course   168
The Crucial Chip   169
Fade or Draw   170
The Radical Open   171
Golf as Mystery   173

INTRODUCTION

Why golf?

No doubt for the deepest anthropological reasons. A small group of hunters—up early—move across the rolling landscape carrying their spears and arrows.

A ritual repeated over and over for centuries. They pause partway for a little something to eat, something to drink, and then push on until returning to the women by nightfall with good news or bad.

The brain feels at home in such circumstances—calculating the odds; choosing the weapon for the intended result. It's happy. And the nostrils breathe in the clear air. The soil is underfoot, and the body is happy too. So why resist it? It is your evolutionary destiny.

And there are other benefits. It's private by contemporary standards. It's playful, and some alliances can be made that help resist an abstract world. It's an ever-changing, absorbing challenge of a kind that blots out problems of a possibly more consequential nature.

It's a kind of heaven—we should be so lucky in the hereafter.

I received my first set of golf clubs from my mother. I was perhaps ten or eleven. I had played a few rounds on the Kenwood Country Club in Cincinnati, Ohio. But it was in another cozy, midwest town, Bloomington, Illinois, where my family's home was a 7-iron across to the twelfth hole of the Bloomington Country Club, that I played for a few years in my teens.

I think I had a good swing. I had some athletic ability, so perhaps my game was better than average; but there were boys I played with who were certainly better golfers. Although I remember reading the article in *Life* magazine detailing Ben Hogan's theory of pronation, and I remember hitting the ball a long way after that.

One summer I went to California and played a lot of par 3 golf, and when I returned to Bloomington, I had for the first time what you could call a golf game. I had hit so many irons in California that I had control; and more important, I was hitting DOWN on the ball, CRUSHING it into the turf, and sending it UP the face of the club over the GROOVES for its TARGET.

That same year I remember playing Gleneagles in Scotland with my father in a light rain, and watching the caddie's eyes light up every time I hit the ball.

Sadly, and I really can't say why, but for all intents and purposes that was the last time I played golf for the next thirty years, until I moved to Hawaii when I was fifty, and began to teach myself the game again. It wasn't a particularly smooth process. I still had a pretty good swing, and some timing from years of other sports, but that's about all. Everything was difficult, and especially scoring well, so I took a radical approach.

Why radical golf?

I had the great pleasure of falling in love again with the game of golf. And in the process, I learned to play the game very differently than I did in my youth. It became obvious to me that the "long" or "big" game—blasting the ball for distance—the game featured on TV and commercials, was not going to be the answer.

I've tried to take the game apart and put it back together again. What follows is what I've learned. I really think I can teach the average golfer how to shoot in the 70s. That's right! And what could be more enjoyable than that?

We will begin by setting our goal for a 79 . . . a 40–39.

One

The Radical Philosophy

The Basic Principles of Radical Golf

Here are some fundamentals which will change the approach to your game pretty drastically. I believe they will make the game far less frustrating—and more in keeping with the true nature of the adventure—and that they will open the paths for scoring well.

Principle Number One

Golf is not a linear game. It's just disguised to look that way.

Scoring is definitely NOT related to advancing the ball as far as possible on each shot.

I prefer to play to areas on the course where you can play your favorite shot, the same shot, the shot you OWN, over and over again.

That's how you take a golf course apart. That's how you dictate to the course, and not vice versa.

And from your favorite areas, you can begin to bomb the green and even the pin.

In basketball, players play from their strengths by going to their favorite spots on the floor.

For instance, Danny Ainge is most comfortable 22 feet from the basket, while Shaquille O'Neal posts up 8 feet away. The defense is geared to keep the player away from his preferred area. But on the golf course there is no one to try to muscle you off the fairway. You just play to your favorite spot.

Perhaps you will want to call it your "free throw" of golf.

Principle Number Two

Keep your mittens on your woods.

You won't be needing them until much, much later. And by then you'll already be scoring in the 70s.

Once you're playing Radical Golf, you'll really only need them on the most demanding courses in the world. And even then, only on certain holes.

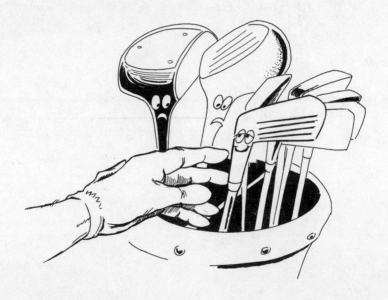

Now it should be stated that if you're a touring professional, and trying to shoot 65, you're going to need to master those dangerous, oddly designed woods.

But you don't need them to shoot a 78.

Taking the mitten off one of those clubs is the beginning of the end for most golfers.

And Principle Number Three

Golf is TWO distinct games, not one.

The first game is played between the tee and the green. If you've paid attention to the first two principles, you've taken a huge step toward mastering Game Number One.

The second game, of course, is putting. We have to learn to get around every nine holes in a lot fewer putts.

My putting recommendations, which are discussed soon, are quite revolutionary—take my word for it.

And there it is. Golf is two games and must be approached that way.

SO REMEMBER, leave the woods at home. Don't be afraid to play short and to position the ball, and the course and this lovely game will begin to bend to your wishes.

How Not to Get Around a Golf Course

Carts mess things up considerably.

Riding, bouncing, drinks sloshing, extra golf balls careening around, the co-rider negotiating the cart path: These things DEFINITELY, DEFINITELY affect your score negatively.

Ride, bounce, get out, practice your swing, hit the ball, get back in the cart, and repeat the process again. This adds 5 strokes, maybe more, to anyone's game.

Walking is the key.

That way, you feel the wind, the dampness of the grass; you see the tilt of the green, the dangerous trap to one side, the overhanging limbs of a tree.

There's no need to think—just let it sink in as you walk. And, oh yes, your arms are swinging—mighty important to your score. And your hips are moving—not frozen on a seat. That alone can destroy your game.

Let someone else drive. Or in an ideal world, of course, play with a caddie.

You can think idly, even talk nonsense as you stroll along. The brain will do the rest pretty much on its own.

One further point—it's nice to have the feeling that you belong in this landscape, that it all makes a kind of sense. It's nice to picture—to imagine—the perfect shot you are to play in the context of the scene.

And remember, the most artistic shot, the most aesthetically pleasing, artfully simple shot, is undoubtedly the best.

WALK, DON'T RIDE.

The Nub of the Big Secret Is Simple Mathematics
Here Is What You've Been Waiting For

A great player, a touring professional, has spent all his time since childhood learning how to play this game. He now plays 320 days a year. He can hit the ball 300 yards. He supposedly has great control with his irons into the greens.

How much better can he score tee to green than you, a Radical Golfer?

I'll show you—not much.

The best touring golfers who have a good solid day will go around nine holes, tee to green, in 19 or 20 shots. A 300-yard drive on the first hole; a 9-iron into the green. A 290-yard drive on the second; a wedge to the green. A 190-yard, tricky par 3, he plops it on the green. Another 300-yard drive, and a wedge. And so it goes. Perhaps he misses the green on the final par 3; but he saves par on this hole and maybe birdies the final par 5. He goes around in 20 shots.

He was up early on the practice tee. He had a seminar with his motivational trainer. Didn't fight with his wife. Hits the ball a ton. It takes him 20 shots, front nine, tee to green.

It takes YOU, the smiling, relaxed Radical Golfer, maybe 23 or 24 shots. I say, give him the three shots!!! This is a pretty good deal, isn't it? A professional quarterback can throw an accurate pass 60 yards; just imagine if you could throw it 51. Or that while Larry Bird might be able to hit 40 free throws in a row, you can hit 33.

You only had to drive 150 to 175 yards on the first hole. To be honest, the yardage really doesn't matter. It took you 3 lazy shots to reach the second hole. You missed the green on the par 3. You played the par 5s conservatively. You hit the short par 3 green. And you went around the nine holes, tee to green, in 23 shots. It might be 24 or 25 shots, but . . .

This is really the big secret. Before you leave home or your hotel room for the golf course, quietly plan how you are going to play the course.

Have a plan—tee to green—BEFORE you tee off.

HOW TO KEEP SCORE

What *Should* Be Listed on Your Scorecard and in the Newspaper

The present scoring system doesn't tell the whole story. Now might be a good time to mention that golf is not really a sport, but a game—or rather, as explained earlier, a combination of two games. It has aspects that are more like chess or checkers—or tiddlywinks, for that matter. Physical conditioning, speed, and hand-eye coordination are not major aspects.

No matter what kind of player you are—a doctor who plays three times a week in the summer or a professional on the tour—you need to understand where you are playing well or poorly. And it is my finding that not listing the number of putts for each nine holes on your scorecard—or in the newspaper, for that matter—is . . . well, to put it politely, a cover-up of the essential aspect of the game. Other sports have expanded their scoring details. Basketball, for instance, has shots attempted, shots made, assists, rebounds, and steals as a matter of course now. And golf needs to move in this direction.

Especially for those who are trying to get a handle on their game.

One reason, perhaps, that they hesitate with golf is that they don't want to admit to the fact that the professional tour is dominated by putting. These players quietly go around, no matter what route they may take, in the same number of shots. They meet on the green and whoever gets hot and rolls in the putts wins.

The Radical Golfer who wants to get his score under control really needs to know the number of putts.

HOLE	1	2	3	4	5	6	7	8	9	OUT
PAR	4	4	3	4	5	4	4	3	4	35
ME (PUTTS)	4 (1)	5 (2)	2 (1)	4 (1)	6 (2)	5 (2)	4 (1)	4 (2)	5 (2)	39 (14)
PETER	5	5	3	4	7	4	6	4	5	43
PAT	6	8	4	5	8	5	5	5	6	52
HARRY	8	6	4	8	7	9	8	4	7	61

HOLE	10	11	12	13	14	15	16	17	18	IN	TOTAL
PAR	4	3	4	5	4	4	3	4	5	36	71
ME (PUTTS)	5 (2)	2 (1)	5 (2)	4 (1)	5 (3)	4 (1)	4 (2)	5 (2)	6 (2)	40 (16)	79
PETER	4	3	6	8	4	6	4	4	6	45	88
PAT	6	3	4	7	6	4	3	6	7	46	98
HARRY	8	5	8	8	7	6	6	9	7	64	125

The last time I shot a 36, for instance, I was 23 shots tee to green and 13 putts.

Follow Me Around Nine Holes
My Last Round of 36. Do You Have These Shots?

Let me describe for you a nice round of 36 on one of the good resort courses in Hawaii—for you to see if you have these shots.

Did I have to make any great shots? Nope. Did I have to roll in any long putts? Nope. Did I hit any long irons into the greens? Nope. Did I hit a 7-iron next to the pin? Nope. Did I hole any of the approaches? Nope. I hate to think of what my score would have been if I had.

Did I have to make some pretty good shots? A few. Some. Was I lucky? You decide.

The first hole. I drive with a 3-iron—a long, easy swing. And then I play an easy 5-iron at the green of this shortish par 4 hole. I may be 5 yards short, and I chip onto the green and make my putt for a 4.

The next hole is a longer par 4 to an elevated green. I drive with my 3-iron. I play a second shot with a 5, and then a pitching wedge into the green from 40 to 45 yards—one of my free throw areas. I am 20 feet from the pin, miss the putt for a 5.

The next hole is a par 3, 165 yards. A 5-iron onto a very large green and I have a good long lag putt and my second putt for a 3.

Are there any tricks so far? Yes. Before leaving home, I have studied the scorecard and I'm familiar with the course. It's revealed to me that I will be needing to hit several solid 5-irons. So on the first two holes, though I could choose from various clubs, I've been setting myself up by playing 5-irons for the crucial shot into the par 3, 165-yard hole. I've been thinking about 5-irons on this round from the beginning, before I teed off.

The next hole is a shortish par 4 and I smack a 2-iron off the tee. Why a 2-iron? Because the following hole is a longish par 5 into some wind and I'm going to be hitting two 2-irons, so I'm setting myself up for the next hole on this par 4. My second shot is a 7-iron onto the fringe of the green and I 2-putt from a reasonable distance for a par.

On the next hole I hit two 2-irons with nice long backswings, low into the wind, and I'm positioning myself for one of the most important shots on this round. A 5-iron. Remember the 5-iron from the first three holes? For a 5-iron into the lowered par 5 green. Did I practice the 5-iron especially before this round? No, I didn't. I don't like to create that kind of pressure. I like to relieve pressure, not create it. I hit a few practice shots before the round, just concentrating on crushing the ball into the turf. I let the clubhead and the design of the club do the rest, and avoid a lot of trouble. This is to a great extent attributable to my not using the awkwardly designed woods and playing the nine holes with the more effective irons. I simply don't need the woods and the length to score well.

By the way, my approach shots on this round were from:

5 yards—a little wedge	*150 yards—a 7-iron*
40 yards—a soft wedge	*the fringe—putting*
the fringe—putting	*5 yards—a little wedge*
the fringe again—putting	*and*
160 yards—the 5-iron	*40 yards—a soft wedge*

Putting and Lag Putting

A truly revolutionary notion—two of them, actually.

First, putting is primarily lag putting. Get the ball close to the hole for a tap-in.

Can you make a 3-foot putt? Or even a 2-foot putt? Fine. Remember *The Manhole Principle*: Once you're on the green, all you have to do is get the ball within 2 feet of the pin. In other words, your target is not a circle 4 inches wide, but one *4 feet wide,* the size of a manhole cover. You don't have to spend minutes laboriously reading the break, kneeling and squinting and testing the earth's magnetic field so your ball swoops down magically into the cup. Just get it within that 4-foot circle. Then take your 2-footer.

And the second secret to putting is unspeakably simple. Take a deep breath before you read further.

Putt with a 2-iron (or a 3-iron if you don't have a 2). You can be deadly from 18 feet, and an accomplished lag putter from much farther out. There it is—that's it. Nobody likes their putters anyway.

Sometimes when I'm playing with friends and a scrunched-over player misses a putt badly, I'll hand him a 2-iron, and it's just crazy how he can roll it in.

There are many technical reasons for this. First of all, you can stand erect, more comfortably over the ball, and with a slightly open stance. Second, the blade is bigger, and grooved, and has more surface to meet the ball. It's a heavier, more comfortable club. It's the right club.

Distance, speed, and control are what we're after. There are just too many putters. Too many designs and lengths, and each weighted differently. It doesn't even sound right when it strikes the ball. *But most of all, it requires a long backswing from a hunched-over position, with frozen shoulders and moving arms.*

Maybe the pros have taught themselves to putt this way, but chances are it's wrong for you. With the iron, you need the shortest possible backswing to "pop" the ball or push it on its course. You'll get a little underspin, which is fine—just as in basketball, tennis, or billiards. Putt like you chip—ball close to you, open stance, a good look at the hole.

It's just a catastrophe that golf developed this stroke on the greens—and that golfers have blithely acceded to it. But I have a friend who recently played his best round of golf, a 65, with only three clubs—a 3-iron, a 5-iron, and a wedge. He putted with his 5-iron—perfectly acceptable, and much better than a screwy putter—but I recommend the 2-iron.

So throw away the putter. Everybody wants to anyway— and this time change to the appropriate club.

––––––

Well, human nature being what it is, I know everyone is going: Whoa! Wait a minute! This is pretty strange. I'm not sure I want to throw away my putter.

So perhaps I should explain further.

I grew up with a very smart group of kids. One of my close friends went to Harvard and MIT at the same time, graduating from both, which you could do in those days. And he has since had a couple of children who graduated from Cal Tech. Anyway, this is a pretty heady family of physicists and mathematicians. When this family was given the task of determining scientifically which club in the golf bag was suitable for accomplishing the job of rolling the ball effectively on the green . . . well, you can figure out which club it *wasn't!*

Sorry to inform everyone, but we've been using the wrong club, and for several hundred years apparently.

Of course, if anyone had just thought about it for a second or two, they could have figured it out. After all, the pros are forever going through fits with this club—changing, redesigning. Bernhard Langer, for goodness' sake, is clamping the putter to his forearm. Someone on the tour is actually putting with one hand. Anyway, there it is, folks. Throw the putter away—this time, far away. I can see the scene across America now. I can hardly wait to hear the deep voice of the English golf announcer on TV as he gets himself around this one. And if you want to hire your own physicists and mathematicians, be my guest.

But just remember, all this is not as crazy as it sounds—

Bobby Jones's famous putter, Calamity Jane, had the loft of a 2-iron. And he putted from an upright position, feet close together.

Following the Four Champions Around

One winter in Hawaii, I was pondering these important golfing questions when the four greatest players in the world came to the island of Kauai—Ian Woosnam, the Masters champion; Ian Baker-Finch, the British Open champion; John Daly, who had won the PGA that summer; and Payne Stewart, who won the U.S. Open.

These fellows would be playing thirty-six holes for something like half a million dollars to the winner. And of course the match would be televised all over the world—to Japan, the United States, and Europe.

It happened to be raining—well, drizzling—but the introductory shots to beautiful Hawaii had been days earlier: sun-drenched surf crashing against the beach, the lush green verdant mountains in the background. The special introductions and promotional material had been taken care of earlier. So when the golf began they just stayed with the players in close-up shots and Hawaii appeared to the world its beautiful self. When I watched later on TV, I thought, Was that the same match I just walked around with?

Now that story, alas, pretty much applies to the way golf is presented on TV and the impression you are given about these great players' games—in stark contrast to your own. Very, very few times on television—almost never—do you see every shot attempted. They traditionally bounce around from player to player, and from the hushed commentary of the announcers you are led to believe that these men with magical swings are controlling the ball as if they had it on a string. "He's just going to fade this shot neatly past the trees on the right and drop it nicely on the green."

Well, these great champions on a 165-yard short par 3—no wind, no huge hazards, a little water to one side—step up to the tee, one after another, and no one hits the green.

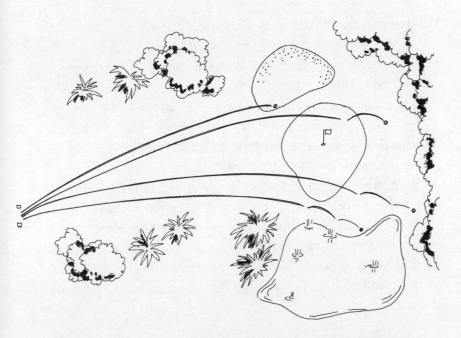

Let me describe to you what this round *was* like. And, by the way, John Daly had a 41 on the front nine. First of all, with their woods, they do *not* hit the ball down the middle. Sometimes they do, but on this wide-open, longish, Jack Nicklaus–designed golf course, these four champions are all over the terrain (although not out of bounds). They do not hit all the greens by any stretch, but they are around the greens and they do get their pars.

On the first hole they play second-shot 6-irons. One is on, three are off. But they get pars. On the fourth, two are in the fairway, two are in a bunker. No one hits the green. Ian Woosnam can only advance his second shot 40 yards, but all get pars!

———

They warm up, they play, they don't know where the ball is going. But they do have very solid, what I call "everyday plateaus"—and then they wait to get lucky. Maybe they will hit a ball close to the pin and make a putt. Maybe they will start rolling in a few long putts. And that's how they score really well. Whoever gets hot, whoever gets lucky, wins. On this day in Hawaii it was Ian Woosnam—the smallest of the four, the last out on the practice tee, but he got hot.

And that's how you want to play, although of course to a different and more conservative "everyday plateau." Nice easy swing down the middle, sometimes a 3-iron, maybe a 2, sometimes a 5, and waiting to hit an approach shot close or roll in a long putt. That's how, the next day, a couple of Radical Golfers had 40s on the same nine holes in the same weather.

Finding Your Own "Free Throw"

Most amateurs and club players already have a shot that they genuinely look forward to—one that they can approach with some confidence. We want to build on that confidence and turn it into arrogance—arrogance based on consistency, of course. It should be an area somewhere inside 150 yards. Many golfers, myself included, feel good about those short par 3 distances; perhaps that's the distance where you feel like a golfer. You swing freely; you take a little turf; you get the ball in the air; it plops on the green. No problem.

Others may look forward to the 80-yard wedge—hard for them to miss the green from this area. Throw the ball up—even the trap in front doesn't seem a worry. Confidence is the key; it brings a freedom to the swing. If you've been walking, that freedom in your swing will come easier.

And I know some cagey fellows who love the area just in front of the greens, prior to those nasty traps. To them the pin, and not just the green, is the target.

So you find your own "free throw." I'll tell you how to get there, and if you begin playing from that spot over and over again, not just once or twice a round, you'll find you'll start scoring. Trust me on this. I saw an old friend from high school recently who asked if I could still hit that 21-foot jump shot from basketball. I told him no, but that I'd found that spot on the golf course.

But it doesn't do you any good to have the good shot and then have rounds where you never use it.

It's simple: If you want to feel like a golfer, this is the key. And another big advantage is that it takes the pressure off the other shots.

Now I've got another news flash for you. All shots during a round are not of the same value. I saw Nick Faldo recently at the British Open drive the ball on a par 5 into a bunker— bad shot number one. He didn't have a lofted enough club to get out—bad shot number two. The ball hit the turf and careened off into the tall grass to his right. Sound familiar? But he hits the next shot—190 yards to the green. Now he's putting for a birdie. He can't stop smiling. He taps in for his par. The *third* shot is the one!

On par 4s the Radical Golfer is only thinking about the third and fourth shots. On par 3s the Radical Golfer is only thinking about the second and third shots. I played recently with my father. He's eighty years old. I drove the 210-yard par 3 green. He's 30 or 40 yards short. But his second shot is a couple of feet from the pin. He plays the 190-yard par 3s short; he plays the 160-yard par 3s short. He concentrates on his second shot. He doesn't worry about the green. He doesn't worry about the traps. He's relaxed. He's talking. What's the worst that can happen? He has to play a wedge from 80 yards. No big deal.

Don't smack the ball.
Play short.
Be cool.
Find your free throw place on the course.

It probably won't be the same as Nick Faldo's—190 yards from the grass—but there's one area where you can consistently put that ball into play on the green. Find it. Then write me and tell me about it.

What to Do When You're *Not* Playing Golf

One of the great pleasures of golf is that it takes some time to play. It eats up a good part of the day. Plus, you've got to get to the course, then visit the nineteenth hole afterward, which, quite seriously, is an important part of the game.

The modern practice of jumping in your car and racing home is not golf. That's part of the "industrial golf phenomenon." You have to tip your caddie, of course, and/or return the cart and tip the young man who handles your clubs. Examining your scorecard while ordering the drinks and a snack is important, and saving the card for study afterward can be good.

Now if you played Radical Golf, chances are you are not so frustrated. You kept the ball down the middle—about the only trouble you would have gotten into is a sand trap around the green. On the whole, your round is a question of how you putted, which you knew before you teed off. And maybe you had a good day and rolled in some putts or hit an approach or two next to the pin, which is the only way to score really well no matter who you are. (We will get to that later in the book.) If you teed off early in the morning, you will now be having lunch. By the time you get home it will be inescapably close to nap time, and that will take you about to the cocktail hour, after which you will be refreshed for the balance of the evening, even if it's only for the news on TV and a quiet supper with a woman who wears dark eye shadow or a man who wears a smoking jacket.

The trouble is—even during the golfing season—chances are you are not going to play golf every day. So the question is what to do on those other days. And I can give the following suggestions:

1. A great newspaper
2. A good breakfast
3. A good lover
4. A great novel
5. A good cigar
6. A wonderful glass of wine or a mixed drink
7. A walk around your neighborhood
8. A wager on another sporting event

9. Some fine music
10. And some business, of course

There's been a lot of talk in my family and among my friends over what is the perfect time to tee off. Early morning is probably great, of course, but my true feeling is that it absolutely doesn't matter as long as you don't have commitments directly afterward. Any commitments. They're the worst.

Some of my friends and I were lucky enough to know Dean Martin when we were younger. He was an avid golfer and totally committed to the game. I always remember the image of him coming in the front door of his home after a bad round and just wanting to get across the hall and up the stairs without questions from his children or his mother-in-law or his wife or anyone. He was told as he was headed up the stairs, "Ricky is sick. Your son has a temperature of 103."

"When it gets to 106, sell!" said Dean Martin as he reached the top of the stairs.

Recapitulation; Where Are We So Far?

We are changing our philosophy about the game. We are walking, those of us who are able to. We have left our woods at home in the garage, unless someone in our family has given us or knitted a particularly attractive set of mittens. We have stored the putter away with the wooden tennis rackets and we are playing short because, unless we are nine years old and just starting out in this game, the chances are we will never have a long game. We are bombing the pin from our "free throw" spots on each hole.

Radical Golf is our deliverance. You can put on your green pin now signifying "I Play Radical Golf."

Two

How to Do It

Most golf books spend all of their time (well, most of it; 95 percent certainly) showing grips, stances, take-aways, and downswings, and never tell how to play the golf course or how to score.

I'm going to reveal what's really important: from how to dress for the game to where to hit your second shot on the 380-yard par 4, up to and including how to get to the nineteenth hole when the round is over.

So here it is—all the essential information.

The Great Leap Forward

I notice when I am away at a remote spot—perhaps on vacation, maybe for work—that the lack of choices in the out-of-the-way place brings quite quickly a certain peace, comfort, routine, serenity. I look forward with great anticipation to the *one* newspaper that arrives rather than rifling madly through scores of magazines and papers as I do at home. I'm relieved by the small number of choices—just the one restaurant; no fifty television channels to select from.

Fewer choices—that's the key. And a lot of Radical Golf's effectiveness, I think, comes from this notion.

It must be stated that although you will have a much better "everyday plateau" and the ability to score really well on many days, you're going to have bad days too. There is no escaping that. Bobby Jones said to himself before each round of golf:

1. *I must be prepared for the making of mistakes.*
2. *I must try to select the shot so as to provide the widest possible margin for error.*
3. *I must expect to do some scrambling, and not be discouraged if the amount represents more than the usual.*

And I've just seen four great PGA players in a round where one player had two double bogeys and another—the leading money winner, to be precise—had six penalty strokes in the same round. These things happen and must be expected. But when disaster does not strike, I know Radical Golf can give you rounds in the 70s. And that, after all, is what we're after.

LOVING THE WEDGE

You've got to love this club. You've got to not be afraid of it. You've got to learn to choke down on it. You've got to learn to open the face. Feel comfortable with this club; have fun with your wedge.

Let's talk about how to use this club from 80 yards; from 40 yards; from 15 or 20 yards.

These crucial strokes are the ones that put the ball into play on the green. These "free throws" can be fun. And they can be made and accomplished by players of all ages and gender. These are the shots that make you feel like a golfer. So here are the essentials for hitting them.

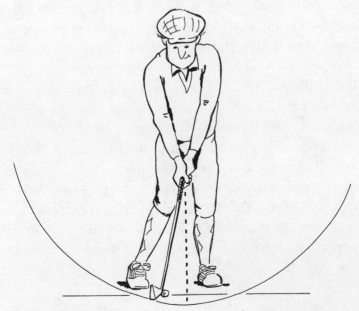

Number One. The hands have to be in front of the ball. That's a definite.

Number Two. Never, ever think about lofting or elevating or scooping the ball. Forget forever that image—the most common mistake of club players. This is another definite: You must hit the ball with a *descending blow*. It's dimple golf. Smack the dimples on the ball on the downward arc of your swing. Let the design of the club do the rest.

Number Three. The ball has to be positioned close to you. And the ball has to be positioned toward the rear of your stance. Later you can place the ball forward, open up the face of the club, put some fancy spin on the ball; but for most wedges, position the ball toward the rear. A nice, slow, firm backswing; watch how slowly the pros take it back. But never decelerate the club on the downswing. Never try for "feel." Swing at it. For 15 yards, for 40 yards—a firm swing. Choke up on the club for control if you like.

Number Four. Obviously, go out and practice from 100 yards, 80 yards, 50, 40, 20.

Picture a three-dimensional object on the green perhaps. Something to amuse you. Perhaps an elephant. Perhaps a house. Picture the ball going in the front door of the house or the upstairs window. Let the club make the shot. Don't be afraid to choke up. Don't try to add "feel" or the club will decelerate on its downswing. These shots take confidence, bravery, but they're the basis for all your fun for years to come.

From 100 Yards Out

Swinging the wedge from 100 yards *is* a little different than with the other irons. Not much, but a little.

From 100 yards you will want to hold the wedge at the end of the club, and it's definitely going to be what could be called a full swing. The classic mistake of the club player is to underestimate the distances for these shots with the wedge.

So. Square up to the ball and be prepared to take a full, forceful swing with the wedge from a distance of 100 yards. And the trick is in the follow-through. Don't stop! A complete, high follow-through is imperative.

So to repeat: Take a full backswing with the clubhead pointing in the direction of the target, then come down forcefully, meeting the ball just before the club reaches its lowest point. Continue past a stable, well-balanced body and head, out and up in a complete follow-through.

Don't quit. Take a forceful swing. You do not want the ball to plop down 20 yards short.

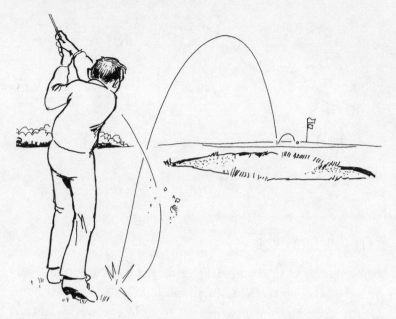

There is this important difference in the swing: It's a steeper take-away than with your long irons. You are not looking to take a big divot, though. Just make the club face meet the back of the ball, generating good backspin as it heads for its target.

Follow-through is for distance and accuracy. Balance is everything.

From 80 Yards Out

From this distance it's the same swing but just a little shorter arc on both sides—the backswing and the follow-through. You square up to the ball the same way, you use the full length of the wedge, you just do not swing quite as force-fully. And the follow-through is still crucial.

From 50 Yards Out

Now things change. You choke down on the club. You flex the knees a little more. It's definitely a smaller arc to the swing, but it's still an enthusiastic swing. It's still a descending blow, of course, and never decelerate.

From 40 Yards Out

I think this is a good distance to make the transition to the sand wedge. This means that with the greater loft you will still be taking a surprisingly healthy swing at the ball. There's often consternation as to when to make the transition from the pitching wedge to the sand wedge. It has to happen sometime, and I think 40 yards is as good a distance as any. And it means you can still take, and indeed must take, an enthusiastic swing. Your follow-through is almost always shoulder high.

From 30 Yards Out

Your grip is lower. You're choking down so your index finger is touching the metal on the shaft, as shown in the next drawing. I think it's a good idea to begin to open up the stance to get a good look at the flag. A shorter swing, a descending blow, backspin, and throw the ball almost all the way to the pin. We are definitely, definitely thinking 1-putt.

From 20 Yards Out

Many golfers have good pitch-and-run shots from this distance. But I still prefer that the Radical Golfer try to "flop" the ball up close to the pin. And if you have a special lofted club for this, use it.

Many times from this distance you are shooting to an elevated green, so then it's definitely the shot. Chipping and rolling the ball on undulating greens of different texture and moisture content just calls for too much knowledge and finesse.

But in all these matters you need to be knowledgeable about your strength, and, ideally, you're playing at the distance at which you are most confident.

That's it. You can have these shots—if you're thirty-five years old, or if you're twelve, or if you're seventy-five.

Learn to love this club. This is the club that's going to be involved in a high number of par 4 third shots. And par 3 second shots. And some par 5 fourth shots.

This is the one that will help you 1-putt. Or 2-putt and prevent the dastardly 3-putt green.

This is the club that makes up for prior mistakes.

> *You and your wedge are one.*
> *If you shoot a 76, this will be why.*

Look sharp and use this club. And then, hell, you're a golfer.

The Moment of Enlightenment

In 1991, I was able to go to Hawaii and devote myself to sporting activities—golf one day, tennis the next—for well over a year. I was without the day-to-day family commitments I'd had for the previous fifteen years or so. I had sold a screenplay to Paramount and was writing another for an actor acquaintance of mine who was filming in China. They wanted me to come to Shanghai, where production was under way—but I was busy on the golf course, trying to get my game in shape. It's a good thing, too, because the producer of that film was gunned down in a volley of bullets by assassins over some dispute. (No doubt what is referred to in the movie business as "creative differences.")

I had uninterrupted time to study the original films of Bobby Jones. I was able to experiment with different clubs for different tasks. . . .

And it was then that it became apparent to me that what it takes to shoot 79s is totally different from what a few talented players at the peak of their prowess need to do to shoot 65s. A player has to be pretty stunning to shoot a 34, but the good news is that you just have to be careful and thoughtful to shoot a 39.

It became obvious that the driving distances, clubs, shot selection, and techniques required for 65 will, in the hands of a club player, absolutely prevent him from shooting 79.

As in life, it became a matter of choices.

Portrait of a Thirty-five-Year-Old Radical Golfer

You may have played some golf over the years; you may have been involved in other sports in school; but now you are established in your career and you're going to want to be playing a lot of golf in the next forty years. That's a long time. So you'll be involved in golf longer than you participated in other sports. It's clear that you are not going to become a professional, but if you're going to play that long you want to be good. Good is having a low handicap. Good is shooting in the 70s. Good is being a consistent, quality player. Well, you know by this point in the book that one critical part of the game is putting, so at the beginning of the golf season you'll want to devote some hours to practice on the putting green. This is a habit you will want to keep each season for years to come. When others see you out on the practice green with your 3-iron, they will know the golf season has begun. The ability to be a great lag putter will make you a great golfer over the years. The people with whom you play will remember you.

Stand straight; get into a slightly open stance; have a good look at the hole; take a short little backswing; flex your knees; don't grip the club too tightly—that's all there is to it. Lag putting is distance, distance, distance. And you want the most compact, simple approach to putting. If you went out each evening before the season and practiced with a normal putting stroke, moving arms, little bit of wrist on the long putts, bent elbows, positioning, aiming, low take-aways, positioning the head—if you didn't have the guru David Ledbetter, you'd be driving yourself nuts. Forget it—*with* David Ledbetter you'd be driving yourself crazy. There's just no way you can become a consistent lag putter with the normal style. I mean, who are we kidding here? You left the office at three o'clock; you're going to practice on the green for an hour; and you're going to play nine holes, maybe eighteen. Then with the golf season under way, you're going to play three, four times a week. You're in desperate need of a simple stroke. The only issue that matters is, do you get around in a lot fewer putts than most? Does your style of play allow you to accomplish this task?

———

You may already travel quite a bit for business or pleasure, and certainly you will in the years ahead. It would be nice to have a lightweight traveling bag for your clubs and to sometimes take just the minimum, which might be your 2, 3, 5, 7, and wedges, your shoes, a golfing costume, good socks (which are so important if you are walking). You will want to get a scorecard as soon as possible for the club you will be playing. How long are the par 3s? How many short par 4s? How long are the par 5s? And then you will be dividing up your shots, tee to green, long before you step out on the course. Naturally, everyone's a little bit nervous on the first tee of a strange course, but you'll be a lot less nervous because you're hitting an iron and a teed-up ball, and that will give you some confidence.

There are some very good rules for the married, thirty-

five-year-old Radical Golfer with family. And I'll just quietly
pass along a couple to you.

Rule Number One. Never leave your home to go directly to
the golf club. Always go from the office. Then return home
after the round of golf. You left for the office, you return
home in the evening. Fundamental.

Rule Number Two. Even if it's Saturday, it's not a bad idea to
go to the office first. But if this is not practical, it's better to
leave before anyone else in the house is awake.

Now, you are probably wondering why I'm mentioning
such matters. We must face facts. If your spouse has been
alone all week with the children, and it's Saturday and you
head out for the golf course, even if she or he is a saint, it's
just possible that the sight of you headed out the door to the
golf club could . . . well, we just have to understand that this
is an issue that must be dealt with. A great deal of emotion
can be involved here, the result of which can be that the
weekend is a disaster—and that the chance to play a game of
golf is completely lost.

From the very beginning, it's essential that golf be seen in
your family as a healthy part of everyone's life and that it
never be called into question. If your children are of school
age, you'll want to fight for their rights to have some un-
structured playtime of their own. You will have noticed that
their life in school is restrictive, mapped out with require-
ments and demands laid down by adults; you'll want your
children to have the joy, the freedom, and the creativity of
unrestricted and unencumbered play. This kind of play is
crucial to the development of the imagination. You are not

going to do anything as a father to spoil this time for your children.

Your spouse, too, deserves some unencumbered playtime of his or her own: tennis, motorcycle riding, gardening, or some other fulfilling outlet. Chances are, he or she will be thrilled to have you gone for several hours. Let the playtime begin . . . and then you'll go play golf.

Golf must not be seen as a threat to your family. Golf must be seen as something you do when the rest of the family is having fun.

Let's Talk About Your Weapons
Your Irons in More Detail

Your long irons, as if you didn't know, are your 2, 3, and 4. What you might not know is that your 2-iron has a loft of 18 degrees, which is a lot more than that of your driver and 3-wood at home in the garage.

Everyone has different distances, of course, and you will learn your own as you play, but your 2-iron will hit the ball about 200 yards and even farther off the tee. So that's pretty okay.

Your 3-iron has a loft of 22 degrees and is designed to hit the ball out there about 190 yards and a little farther off the tee. Your 4-iron has a big loft of 26 degrees for 180 yards. These clubs can get that ball up in the air.

These are your long irons. You're going to hit these clubs twelve or thirteen times every nine holes, so it's good to get acquainted with these weapons.

Now, by the way, I hate, really hate, the new rubberized handles that can tear your hands up and require one of those gloves that have to keep going on and off. Leather handles can and should be put on your clubs—very inexpensively, at maybe $9 per handle.

Can you imagine tennis pros taking off their leather grips and then putting on a rubber one so you have to wear a glove? Who thinks of this stuff?

Your medium irons are your 5, 6, and 7. And their loft will

be 30 degrees, 34 degrees, and 38 degrees. You see, every club has a loft difference of 4 degrees. Its flight path is, therefore, a little higher and about 10 yards shorter. Your 5-iron is made to go about 170 yards, your 7-iron about 150. You can hit greens with these clubs if you have to. They're especially important for a lot of par 3 and 5 holes. These are clubs you should learn to have faith in. You can position the ball with them; generally it's going to go where you want. These are confidence clubs, and they are the ones you want to play with.

Your short irons are your 42-degree 8-iron and your 46-degree 9-iron. These two short irons are for the 130- to 140-yard range.

Now by all means don't worry if you hit these clubs to shorter distances than those just mentioned. It couldn't matter less. This is just important background information so that you know how the club is designed. All of these clubs can position a ball nicely no matter what ground you have to cover. And the alternative is to play with 10- and 15-degree lofted clubs and have to hit them fourteen and fifteen times every round. As I've said before, they will send your score soaring. They are obstacles.

All right, now the wedges, the clubs we are passionate about.

The pitching wedge with a loft of 50 degrees is good for 110 yards down to about 80 or 90, where the sand wedge takes over. This club is sharply lofted at 56 degrees, 6 degrees more than the pitching wedge. It really throws the ball up high and it's just so effective around the greens.

Now let's make one thing very clear: Many, many country-club golfers do not own a sand wedge. If you are going to play Radical Golf, you have to go out and *buy one.* It's a tremendous advantage, not only out of the sand but from many spots on the fairway. These wedges are the clubs for a large part of this game's adventure. And it should be noted that, like the other irons, they are not bounded by differences of 10 yards in their ranges. The wedges combined have an 80-, 90-, out to a 120-yard range.

> *In Radical Golf you are playing over and over again to the area of your wedge.*

The Most Overlooked Aspect of the Game of Golf

It simply is that the ball is stationary, just sitting there . . . waiting. The ball's not moving. *Nothing* is moving to excite the eye and the muscles, as in other sporting activities.

That's what this damn preparation routine you see the pros go through is all about. That's what the "forward press" is about. To compensate for the fact that the ball is just sitting there . . . waiting.

You see, the brain needs a little trick to send the electrical charge down to the muscles. This is why tennis pros take little hop steps when they're waiting to receive serves.

So first you need a waggle—a movement, just a touch, a little routine, but don't think it ain't important. It's crucial.

It is the most individual game—just you and the ball . . . but it's seldom played alone. A contradiction: You are isolated, but with other people. You play your shot while others watch.

It's not really golf if you're by yourself. If no one sees or hears the tree fall in the forest, it didn't. If you play your approach to the green and it backs up next to the hole and no one is there to see it . . . well, you get the point.

So to this degree, golf is a performance. Not enough club players understand this.

The same could be said about life. I *will* say it. The individual alone has no meaning separate from his family, kin, or community. The idea that there is an individual separate from his relationships is just fallacious.

    ——

Hence the importance of etiquette in golf, as in life. He who is farthest from the hole plays first. On the green, he who is farthest from the pin putts first. He who has the honors hits first on the tee. You replace your divots in the fairway; you rake the sand. You don't step on your colleague's putting line. You don't interrupt with talk while he's playing. You don't move in his eyeline. This is all part of the game—make it part of yours.

    ——

Golf is like *placekicking* in football. You see, it's down. It's placed. It's there. The kicker has to repeat the perfect action. His teammates don't talk to him on the sidelines before he has to do it. It's odd. No one isolates the halfback before he goes in. No one isolates the receiver before they send him in for the crucial first down.

Golf is like placekicking seventy-eight times a round. Thank God for the gimme putts. For the tap-ins.

In basketball, the brain is constantly calculating and adjusting for your speed, your jump, the pace of the ball, the open teammate behind you. The brain loves this stuff and is excited by it. But it's different in golf. It's like placekicking, and you have to recognize this. Of course, the more you can make your approach to a green from *a repeatable distance,* the better. The more it's like an extra-point kick. The more you can *routine it off.* This is the feeling you are looking for.

I hope this puts it all in some perspective. You see, if the little ball was moving, your brain would get that clubhead straight at impact, as it does with the racket face in tennis. But it's not moving. It's just there. It's golf.

The Medium Irons

Okay. We're going to widen our stance a bit for balance and position the ball a little more forward. So these two things will be different.

But it is still a descending blow—with irons we *never* try to sweep the ball—and our weight moves to the left leg. That should do it. And it's still important to have that lazy backswing. In the rough, hold the club tighter.

The Long Irons

You'll be hitting with these clubs a lot from the fairway and off the tee. So here's all you need to know: left arm straight—you've heard that before. Left arm take-away, and a long—be sure of this—a *long* backswing for clubhead speed. And remember, get your left side out of the way, and as usual, smack it with a descending blow.

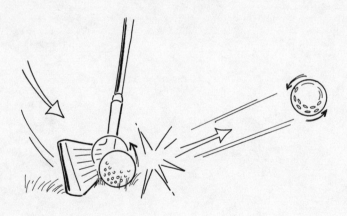

Okay, that's it; the lesson's over.

Remember that for good, traditional, professional golfers, *every* shot is hit with underspin, except when using the driver and the putter. Of course, we Radical Golfers are putting with 2-irons, which gives us a little bit of backspin on the green.

Our 2-irons, our 3-irons, our 5-irons, whether off the tee

or off the fairway, are hit with long backswings, but impact is always made at the bottom of the swing. Always. Otherwise, the ball would not have the needed backspin to climb into the air. And the backspin gives us accuracy.

———

I suppose you should know this: When you're hitting these shots really well, it's a special feeling—yes, a sweet-spot feeling.

> **The sweet spot is easier to find when you hit with a descending blow.**

Exaggerate the idea in practice until you find this feeling. But don't expect to have it all the time. Be reasonable. Don't be too hard on yourself.

When to Play Short? When to Hit It!

Well, the answer to the first question is *almost always*—that is, if you want to break into the 70s consistently. There are only a few reasons to hit the ball for distance. On a par 5 you'll want a long, full backswing with your 2- or 3-iron off the tee on your first fairway shot; you'll want to bring the leg muscles and back muscles into play. Other than that there's no real need to smack the ball. On the long par 4s you can really play awfully short with your first two shots because you're just trying to position your ball nicely for your third shot. Even on a pretty short par 4 I'm usually for playing short in front of the green and in front of what are often dangerous traps. On the longish par 3s I'm in favor of playing short for the same reason.

Why play short? Because we want our scorecard to look like this: 4, 5, 3, 4, 5, 4, 3, 4, 4—which is one of our goals of 36. Or 5, 5, 4, 4, 6, 4, 3, 4, 4, which is a 39 (with a 6 and only parring one par 3).

You are playing short to eliminate blunders. You are playing short to establish a solid "everyday plateau" from which, on some days, you can get hot by hitting wedges next to the pin or by rolling in some putts with your trusty 3-iron.

> REMEMBER THIS . . . *golf is a secret language made up of what shots are NOT played as much as by what shots are.*

Success, Failure, and Golf
A Round of Golf Facts

1. Bob Hope plays golf.
2. Bing Crosby played golf.
3. The Japanese play golf.
4. The Americans play golf.
5. The Germans play golf.
6. Michael Jordan plays golf.
7. Hitler didn't play golf, but
8. Ike did.
9. Katharine Hepburn played golf.
10. Howard Hughes played golf, and he played with Katharine Hepburn.
11. Fred Astaire played golf.
12. Jackie Gleason played golf, but
13. Richard Nixon did not, *really*.
14. George Bush played a little golf, and
15. Saddam Hussein does not.
16. Of course, Bobby Jones played golf.
17. And Jack William Nicklaus plays golf.
18. And so do you.

Your Fiancé, Your Spouse, Your Marriage, and Golf

If your spouse understands about golf, your marriage can last. If your spouse ridicules the game or is threatened by it, then you're going to have lots of grief. If your spouse recognizes its charm, its beauty, its pastoral qualities; the challenge, the discipline, the thoughtfulness, the harmony of the game . . . well then, there is probably a glow around your spouse's head, if you look closely.

But if your spouse sees it as inane, as unproductive, as time-wasting, you are truly in the deepest, heaviest rough.

It's a litmus test, friends! Maybe the best one there is.

Golf Is Really Par-Three Golf!

The heart of the matter is that all golf is really par 3 golf. All holes are par 3 holes of various lengths. The big question is: What lengths? The difference between the professional and the Radical Golfer is simply that the professional has to play his approach shots from much greater distances. The Radical Golfer is *willing to give up more strokes* to put the ball in play to the green (free throws) from shorter and better-located situations. The professional blasts the ball to get within his range. As stated earlier, for a club player this is absolutely not necessary in order to score in the 70s. All you have to do is accept this easy solution.

If you can't consistently drive 235–300 yards, you are going to use *two shots* to place the ball in position, and probably three on a par 5.

The need to hit a wood disappears forever. Well, almost. Certainly for the foreseeable future, anyway.

So now it just becomes a matter of choosing the most conservative and best-lofted club to accomplish this task.

The Big Challenge

For the doubters, the big doubters, here's a challenge. Play a round with just a 7-iron off the tee and fairways, then a wedge, and putt with a 3-iron on the green. I'm saying you'll score better than you do now, unless you are already hovering around the cusp of the 70s. On the 420-yard par 4, play *three* 7-irons. On the 318-yard par 4, play *two* 7-irons and a wedge. On a 185-yard par 3, a 7-iron and a wedge. On the 420-yard par 4, *two* 7-irons and a wedge. Lots of 7-irons. No 3s, no 5s, no woods. On the long par 5—560 yards—*three* more 7-irons and a wedge. Keep 'em coming. Maybe you'll be able to hit the short par 3 in 1. In any event, it's only 26 shots tee to green. If you miss the short par 3, it's 27. Big deal. Do you see how this works? With a 7-iron, you're only 3 shots more than our goal of 23. You're going to make some putts, and you're going to score 41, 42, 43. Something like that. And that is probably a lot better than what you're doing now, trudging out there with that big bag of clubs. So accept this challenge. Try it with a friend. Try it more than once. See what this game is really like. It's not that difficult. You'll soon be hovering around the low 80s . . . and this is just an exercise! You can build your game from here—lengthening your irons one step at a time. Start today!

Who said this wasn't Radical Golf?

Portrait of a Sixty-four-Year-Old Radical Golfer

You may think you are too set in your ways to change. You like your woods—your 5-wood, your 7-wood—and you don't feel the need to be any kind of revolutionary.

Or worse, you might think that going out without woods is a sissy thing to do. After all, you remember Slammin' Sammy Snead.

Clint Eastwood is just about your age. Not only is he at the height of his powers as a filmmaker and actor, but he has had the very good sense to live in Carmel, California. He probably still plays with his woods—until he reads this book, because Clint, although true to his principles, is also still at the cutting edge. After all, he's a new father, and what could be more cutting edge than that! So don't be lazy. Don't be a grumpy old conservative. Just try it. Blast that 3-iron off the tee and start taking shots off your scores. Look at the game differently. Look at your wedge differently. Study the scorecard at home. See if you can go around in 24 shots, 14 putts. If you're chipping well from in front of the green, and you give that 3-iron a try, you too can be at the height of your powers (and, who knows, maybe there'll be a new baby in your life, too). Go for it. The game deserves it. You deserve it.

A Bad Round of Golf

Before we go any further, let's look at a bad round. Let's see where the trouble grows and what you've been using for fertilizer to make sure it grows.

Your scorecard when you're finished looks like this: 6, 5, 5, 6, 5, 7, 6, 4, 6. A 50! Oh my God! But don't worry—help is on the way.

You drove down the right side right behind some big trees. You had to play down to the other side of the fairway into some light rough. Your approach was short; your chip was onto the green but way short of the pin. And you 2-putted. This is classic. I see it all the time. You handled the green okay by 2-putting, but the *third and fourth shots* were completely ineffective. The approach shot was short; the chip was short.

Believe me, you could have survived even with your awkward drive and second shot.

The second hole you played gave you a little bit of encouragement, but then on the par 3 you hit the ball under trees to the left of the green. Now you had to get the ball on the green, keeping it down under the trees. You were *short of the green on your second shot;* you *chipped badly,* so your poor second and third shot gave you a double bogey 5.

Any short, straight shot on the par 3 to have given yourself a chance to hit a second shot into the green would have been preferable.

You HAVE TO protect your second shot on the par 3s.

On the fourth hole, you drove the ball well. You felt like a golfer. You hit a wonderful second shot. You were in a position to hit your approach. Your wedge wasn't bad. Short. On the fringe. Chip uphill. No good. You 3-putted for a 6. So the early good shots meant nothing.

My gosh, after four holes you used 22 shots. But as awkwardly as you played off the tee and the fairway, you could have been putting for 4s and a 3 with a good wedge.

On the next par 4 you were discouraged but determined to turn your game around. You were tempted by the green and hit your second shot into the trap. On the par 5, you crisscrossed the fairway back and forth; you reached the green in 5; your putt rimmed the cup, and you tapped in for a 7. On the long par 4 you were frustrated. You reached the green in 4 and 2-putted for a 6.

On the last holes you weren't betrayed on the greens particularly; you were betrayed by your woods. Gee, you used 40 shots after seven holes. Sound familiar? And if you analyze it, all you really needed was *a pretty good wedge*. And to *get rid of those woods*. You could have been approaching the eighth hole, the par 3 coming up, with a score of 33 rather than being hopelessly out of sorts and clinging to the idea that the next nine holes would be different.

Let's look at some examples of how to turn things around.

Riding the Escalator Down: Two Scorecards

	FRIDAY				SUNDAY		
Hole	Tee to green	Putts	Total	Hole	Tee to green	Putts	Total
1	4 .	3 =	7	1	3 .	2 =	5
2	3 .	3 =	6	2	3 .	2 =	5
3 (par 3)	3 .	2 =	5	3	2 .	2 =	4
4	3 .	2 =	5	4	3 .	2 =	5
5	3 .	2 =	5	5	3 .	1 =	4
6 (par 5)	4 .	3 =	7	6	4 .	2 =	6
7	3 .	3 =	6	7	3 .	2 =	5
8 (par 3)	3 .	2 =	5	8	2 .	2 =	4
9 (par 5)	4 .	2 =	6	9	4 .	2 =	6
	30 .	22 =	52		27 .	17 =	44

We could have gone out on Friday for your 52 and been able to score 44 on Sunday. You guessed it—we got rid of the woods!

On Sunday, we only used 3 shots rather than 4 on the first par 4, and we 2-putted for a 5, and we played the second par 4 the same way. That's really our goal: 3 shots on a par 4, tee to green, chip on and 2-putt. And that's what we've done.

And we played the par 3 short, chipped on, 2 putts, and

got our 4. So we've got a little formula going.

The next par 4, it's 3 shots down the middle, onto the green, and a 2-putt for a 5.

On the fifth hole we're going to get our first par, because we play our 3 shots, it's a short par 4, we're right up close to the edge of the green, and we're able, for the first time, to chip on close enough to the pin to make the putt.

We play the next par 5 very conservatively—4 shots, 2-putting—and stick with our formula the rest of the round for our 44.

We used 2 shots to get to the green on the par 3s and 4 shots to get on the par 5s; we used 3 shots to get on the par 4s; we 2-putted every green but one. And one hole we chipped close enough to get down in 1, for a round of 44. This is bogey golf. A comfortable plateau. It's nice to have the one par where you chip close. Now we will build on that idea.

Several days later, a new scorecard:

Hole	Tee to green		Putts		Total
1	3	.	2	=	5
2	3	.	1	=	4
3 (par 3)	2	.	1	=	3
4	3	.	2	=	5
5	2	.	2	=	4
6 (par 5)	4	.	1	=	5
7	3	.	2	=	5
8 (par 3)	1	.	2	=	3
9 (par 5)	3	.	2	=	5
	24	.	15	=	39

Wow! We're five strokes better.

What's different here? We can hit a straight 7-iron or 6-iron. We've only added a couple of talents to our repertoire.

We've learned how to play the par 3s conservatively. We've parred both of them. On the short par 3 we hit the green and 2-putted; on the longer par 3 we played short and chipped up next to the hole for a 3. We've learned how to play the par 3s. We chipped close enough to 1-putt three times. That's it!

Another day, two more strokes off.

Hole	Tee to green		Putts		Total
1	3	.	2	=	5
2	3	.	1	=	4
3 (par 3)	1	.	2	=	3
4	3	.	1	=	4
5	2	.	2	=	4
6 (par 5)	4	.	1	=	5
7	2	.	2	=	4
8 (par 3)	1	.	2	=	3
9 (par 5)	3	.	2	=	5
	22	.	15	=	37

Well, we're still not rolling in any long putts, but we're chipping up close from around the green. And now we can hit pretty consistently 5-, 6-, and 7-irons.

Here's what we're not doing. We're not killing the ball off the tee with Big Bertha. We're not hitting any long irons into the green. We're not bombing the green with any short irons. We're laying up and know how to chip!

How to Dress for Golf

This could be a controversial chapter . . . more than the one about keeping the mittens on your woods . . . more than the one about putting with your 3-iron. This could be where the reader thinks about throwing the book across the room. But maybe not.

Here's what some players look like on the tour now. Today a lot of them play in spite of their costumers.

Perhaps Seve Ballesteros knows how to dress for golf. After all, he's Spanish and he doesn't have some ridiculous hat on his head. Maybe Gary Player knew once. Jack Nicklaus has been pretty good about not putting some dumb thing on his head.

In the past, of course, there were wonderfully dressed golfers. And old photographs of them can be a pretty good guide to what you should wear.

A safe rule, probably, is that you can't wear artificial fibers on a grassland dotted with trees. Maybe in a concrete-and-glass city, but not in Scotland or Ireland or on your own golf course. It just looks dumb . . . and must feel dumb too.

So wool or cotton—that's pretty much it in the fabric department. Cotton for the hot summers and wool for the brisk temperatures. And they should be fairly loose and easy for swinging and hitting the ball.

With all the catalogues now available, organizing these clothes is a lot easier than it used to be. And the stuff comes directly to your door, which is about as convenient as it can get. Pringle still makes good cashmere. Perhaps the best cotton golf shirts are the Bobby Jones brand, Lyle and Scott, and Lacoste, since they've been bought back by the original French company. Zanella trousers from Italy are good. Surprisingly, the best golf shoes are made by Ralph Lauren: Polo.

Baseball caps make sense on a baseball field; plantation hats look really good on a coffee plantation. Tom Kite is too short to wear a big straw hat with something written all over it. I think he would win more tournaments with a nice tweed cap, or even sunscreen. It's also nicer and more comfortable to take off your golf shoes after a round, slip into your loafers, and not look like an idiot if you stop somewhere on the way home after a round.

But what's all this dressing business got to do with playing well? Unfortunately, everything! It's all tied in with respect for the game. And that's why Jose Maria Olazabal is probably a better golfer than John Daly. Fred Couples, of course, looks good, plays well. John Cook looks good. Nick Faldo looks wonderful; Faldo wins. Quite simply, the better you dress, the better you score, the more money you win. It's weird, but that's the way it works. Now sure, there are exceptions that prove the rule, but why torture yourself and others?

Jerry Rice, the National Football League's greatest receiver of all time, arrives at the stadium hours early to dress for the game. Everything must be perfect. He's meticulously dressed; he runs meticulous pass patterns. He's the greatest. And, oh, by the way, the first time that Andre Agassi, with all his individualistic-expressionistic costumes, ever won a Grand Slam tennis event was Wimbledon—where he had to wear white . . . and grass isn't even his best surface. Say what you will, it's all connected.

Dress well—play well.

Thinking Your Way Around the Course

The Front Nine at Pebble Beach

Once you're dressed, the next order of business is to think your way around the course. BEFORE you walk out with your clubs. Let's look at the challenging opening hole of Pebble Beach as an example of how to break a course down.

Look at the par 3s first. On the front nine at Pebble Beach there are two short par 3s—one 166 yards, one 107, the latter overlooking the ocean. You might be able to hit both of these greens, but let's go for one and play one short.

Look for any really short part 4s. There's one here, a shortish par 4—327 yards. Good deal. You could go for it in 2, or play short.

Now let's look at the par 5s. It's a famous course; let's play them conservatively and use 4 shorts tee to green.

Okay, that leaves the balance of the par 4s. Check them out carefully, taking caution to stay away from the bunkers. The eighth and ninth holes are very special; this is where Pebble Beach starts becoming a tough course.

Okay, here's the deal: I think you can get around in 25, maybe 26 shots tee to green. And if you go around in 14 or

15 putts, that's a 39 or 41. Not bad on one of the most famous courses in the world.

HOLE	BACK rated 74.4 / slope 142	MIDDLE rated 72.1 / slope 138	PAR						HANDICAP	FORWARD rated 71.9 / slope 130
1	373	338	4						8	322
2	502	439	5						10	363
3	388	341	4						12	275
4	327	303	4						16	256
5	166	156	3						14	140
6	516	487	5						2	385
7	107	103	3						18	88
8	431	405	4						6	350
9	464	439	4						4	330
OUT	3274	3011	36							2509
PLAYER										
10	426	395	4						7	296
11	384	374	4						5	316
12	202	184	3						17	166
13	392	373	4						9	285
14	565	553	5						1	420
15	397	366	4						13	308
16	402	388	4						11	307
17	209	175	3						15	164
18	548	538	5						3	426
IN	3525	3346	36							2688
TOT	6799	6357	72							5197
HANDICAP										
NET SCORE										
DATE		SCORER					ATTEST			

THE RADICAL GOLFER VS. TOM WATSON

Let's examine our Radical Golfer in the worst possible situation. He's going to play the devilish and torturous *back nine* at Pebble Beach right along with Tom Watson the year he won the U.S. Open, 1982—the exact round, hole by hole. One can actually score on the front nine at Pebble Beach, and later we will talk about how this might be done. But the back nine is another matter altogether. So let's see what might happen.

The tenth hole. Tom Watson drives 275 yards. Ouch! The Radical Golfer is worried by the narrow fairway. He plays a 5-iron only 160 yards. Hmm. Watson has outdriven us by *115 yards* off the tee.

The Radical Golfer plays a 3-iron off the fairway 175 yards. That still leaves an 80-yard wedge to the green. Surprisingly Watson's 7-iron is way to the right of the green, but he recovers out of tall grass to about 25 feet from the pin. Well, we play our wedge 35 feet from the pin. And because Tom Watson is a great competitor, he actually *makes his 25-foot putt* and saves par, while we 2-putt from 35 feet. Tom takes a 1-stroke lead. We can live with that.

On the eleventh, 384-yard blind driving hole, it's necessary to stay left. Tom crushes his drive and he plays a little approach 22 feet from the pin. Hardly seems fair. The Radical Golfer is so far behind it's not funny, and he plays his second shot still 40 yards short of the green. The Radical Golfer hits a nice shot from the 40-yard distance, 20 feet from the pin—a good "free throw." Oh, gosh, Watson actually rolls in his *second* putt in a row. The Radical Golfer 2-putts for a 5 and Tom has his birdie and a 3-stroke lead. It's okay. Watson can't keep this up.

On the 207-yard par 3, Watson plays for the green, but hits his ball into a bunker. This can happen. With our Radical Golfer's conservative play—short in front of the traps—he is able to chip up to 15 feet away, the same distance as Tom's shot out of the sand. Now the Radical Golfer seeks revenge and rolls in a 15-foot putt with his trusty 3-iron. Tom, un-nerved by this, rims the cup for a bogey. The Radical Golfer recovers a stroke and the two golfers move to the thirteenth hole. We can play this game.

On the thirteenth hole, another par 4, Watson sends the ball farther than we've ever seen anyone drive the dimpled sphere—way past 300 yards on the left side of the fairway. Somehow we manage to play short, down the middle, and hit a second shot 40 yards in front on the left. Tom plays his second-shot wedge to the green; we play our third shot to the green. He 2-putts again; so do we. We lose another stroke to one of the world's great players, and are 3 down again as we move to *the fourteenth hole.*

A real horror of horrors. It's a *par 5, 565-yard hole.* With Tom's length off the tee, he will certainly kill us on this hole. And he has a long, long drive off the tee. But Tom doesn't consider going for the green in 2. He lays up with a 5-iron. The Radical Golfer plays two 2-irons, leaving him still a long 5-iron away. Tom hits his third shot 35 feet from the pin; the Radical Golfer hits his third 10 yards short of the green and chips on 8 feet away from the pin, laying 4. But my God! *Now we watch Watson roll in another 35-foot putt for a birdie.* That's the third long putt he's made. Our Radical Golfer is lucky to make his 8-foot putt and save a par. Watson leads by 4. When are we going to make our move?

The fifteenth, 397-yard par 4—we're into it now. Our adrenaline is pumping. He hits a huge drive. He's so far out there it's frightening. So we hit a 2-iron 190 yards; we hit a second 3-iron and we're still 15 yards in front of the green. He's taken out his wedge and, plunk, he's 15 feet from the pin. This guy is unrelenting. But the Radical Golfer has his resources and bombs the pin from just off the green. The ball trickles 9 feet past the hole. Tom misses his 15-foot putt and takes a par. Luck is with us. The Radical Golfer sinks the 9-footer—*that's two good putts in a row for us.* We're still 4 down as we move to *the sixteenth.*

Tom thinks about playing a 3-wood here, but decides he needs to play for a birdie, so he crushes another drive and buries it in a fairway bunker. He should have played the 3-wood. The Radical Golfer doesn't have this problem. He poops it out there, hits his second shot, and is still 80 yards from the green. Watson comes out of the bunker to the fairway, then hits his third shot 50 feet past the hole. Our wedge is 30 feet from the hole. We're holding our own against this guy now. He 2-putts for a bogey. This is our chance. But we 2-putt for a bogey. And we have two holes to play.

The seventeenth is a par 3, 209 yards. Tom hits a 2-iron and misses the green. We play the hole short, of course, avoiding the traps; we chip up nicely. But wouldn't you know it? This guy actually chips his approach in the hole for a birdie. Well, he's not called Tom Watson for nothing.

We did okay the last three holes—two pars and a bogey. Not bad!

The lovely finishing hole is along the ocean. Tom's going to come in with a 34 or 35, but you know, we're going to come in with a 39 or 40. Not all that bad. I mean, he has killed us off the tee; it's been all the Radical Golfer could do to hold his head up. And he's killed us on the greens. He's rolled in 3 long, long putts and, my gosh, he even sank an approach.

Of course, Tom Watson won the Open, but we had a nice round. We enjoyed being out there. We made a couple of putts. We demonstrated our nice, solid, conservative "everyday plateau."

And of course we're thinking later in the evening, when we shut our eyes just before falling asleep—What if WE had rolled in the 35-foot putts? What if WE had holed our approach from off the green . . . and he hadn't? We might have beaten Tom Watson. . . .

It's a lot better than counting sheep!

A Review of the Match

The Radical Golfer is taller than Tom Watson. But that's about all. Watson has won the British Open three times. He's won the Masters twice. And, of course, he's won the U.S. Open. He knows the course at Pebble Beach well. I think he went to Stanford and used to motor down and play a round in the morning before classes. He outdrove the Radical Golfer by hundreds of yards. But . . .

Tom Watson used 22 shots tee to green and 13 putts for his 35. He 1-putted three greens and sank another approach.

The Radical Golfer used 25 shots tee to green and 14 putts for his 39.

Tom had to play almost every day since he was nine for his 4-stroke victory.

And to complete the profile of the match, the Radical Golfer's approaches were from 80 yards, 40 yards, 15 yards, 40 yards, 10 yards, 15 yards, 80 yards, 20 yards, and 135 yards.

Ranking the Shots

As must be obvious by now, all shots are not equal in this world of golf. So for once and for all time, we are going to rank them in order of importance. There will be those out there who disagree with us, but we can live with that.

The *drive* doesn't matter. It matters a little on a par 5, but just a little. The second shot on a longish par 4 doesn't really matter. It matters more than the drive, but the third shot *really* matters! We can debate this forever, but . . .

It's the **third shot** *on a par 4 that counts for everything.*

The first shot on a short par 3 matters. The first shot on a medium par 3 matters. But . . .

It's the **second shot** *on the par 3s that really count.*

And

It's the **third and fourth shots** *on the par 5s that are everything.*

Memorize all of the above and you'll be a lot more relaxed and know just what to practice.

Now it's here that we disagree with Harvey Penick's wonderful *Little Red Book*. He discusses with Herbert Warren Wind which are the three most important clubs, and of course Mr. Penick believes that it's a putter, a wood, and a wedge. Well, of course, I disagree completely with the putter, because it's the wrong club and shouldn't be in the bag. And of course I disagree with the wood, because it should never be pulled out of the bag except in dire emergencies. So, needless to say, that leaves as the three most important clubs the wedge, the wedge, and the wedge.

The Teenage Radical Golfer

Thirteen- or fourteen-year-olds can become wizards with the wedge and lag putters supreme with their 3-irons. The skill and, yes, the fun can be more satisfying than skateboarding and more exciting than a first date. Fresh air, the outdoors, several hours away from television, a game that can be played with peers or intergenerationally. As in tennis, a four-teen-year-old can compete with any age group. Not a lot of strength is required; teenagers have more than enough. But I must stop now or courses everywhere will be suddenly flooded by a new, young crowd.

Golf, and especially Radical Golf, emphasizes judgment and shrewdness over dumb power. Radical Golf provides the plateau for assessing the potential of a really talented golfer. A good swing learned early goes a long, long way, but nothing is as satisfying as a "free throw" learned early. For young women, by the way, it's almost an automatic scholarship to a university, so a little Radical Golf should be integrated with studies and dates. And universities *will* come calling. In what can be a pretty crazy world, what could be better than a daughter devoted to the game of golf? As a teenager, I knew a girl who flew an airplane and had a wonderful golf swing—a pretty dazzling combination. And she was pretty. She's flying around the Caribbean playing golf right now.

Of course, southern kids traditionally make great golfers, but golfers come from everywhere, even Sweden and Paraguay. So get onto this great game.

Mapping the Course

We shouldn't wait any longer. Here is the primer—the formula—for setting the strategy for each course long before you tee off.

Take a deep breath. I think you will be surprised at how fundamentally you can influence the level of your score even before you leave the clubhouse. First, you want to use, if possible, 23 shots—tee to green—on nine holes. This can vary by features such as the length of the par 3s and if there are one or two par 5s. You may need 24 or 25 or 26 shots for the round—no problem. But you must know your goal beforehand. And have worked it out in your head—or better, on the scorecard itself.

On the back nine in Hawaii where I shot a 36, I used 23 shots; at the other end of the spectrum would be the back nine at Pebble Beach, where I used 26 or maybe 27.

So you apportion your shots playing short in front of fairway bunkers and ominous green-side traps.

But here's the most important part of the format. Remember where I played my approaches from on the Hawaiian course? I'll remind you.

On four holes I was within 10 yards of the green. On two holes I was within 40 yards and on three holes I was beyond the 40-yard mark at approximately 150 to 165 yards away.

Now on the back nine at Pebble Beach, which is a hell of a challenge by any standard, the Radical Golfer played his free throws as follows:

> **Three from the 40-yard mark, five from 20 yards and closer, and two from 80 yards.**

Not bad! So before a round of golf, it's your wedge that you emphasize in your practice session from these appropriate distances, and it's this club that will protect your "everyday plateau" and give you consistency. And if you get hot with this club and your 3-iron on the green, that will enable you to tear the course apart.

How to Break Down a Course for Playing a Round

Since I can't offer you your home course scorecard, here is Cypress Point, one of the most imaginative courses ever built anywhere. So study the following, make your choices, and I'll have some comments afterward.

Hole 1 418-yard par 4

Hole 2 551-yard par 5—bunkers, lots of them, from 50 yards into the green

Hole 3 161-yard par 3—a shortish hole with bunkers between you and the green

Hole 4 385-yard par 4—bunkers from 100 yards and in

Hole 5 491-yard par 5—a short par 5 but tons of bunkers almost the entire route

Hole 6 522-yard par 5—bunkers around the green

Hole 7 163-yard par 3—shortish hole; green surrounded by bunkers

Hole 8 355-yard par 4—dogleg

Hole 9 291-yard par 4—remarkably short

A pretty short nine holes; a par 37 because of the odd configuration of three par 5s. The back nine, coming in:

Hole 10 491-yard par 5—some bunkers

Hole 11 434-yard par 4

Hole 12	409-yard par 4—dogleg and bunkers
Hole 13	362-yard par 4
Hole 14	383-yard par 4
Hole 15	130-yard par 3—short but magical and followed by the odd configuration of two par 3s back-to-back
Hole 16	233-yard par 3—a big carry across water; an extremely dramatic hole
Hole 17	375-yard par 4—dogleg
Hole 18	342-yard par 4—an easy finish

Two Radical Golfers—Pat and Mike—a woman in her thirties and a man in his forties—set out to play Cypress Point. There's some wind, a little morning mist, and it sprinkles on and off during the front nine. Mike is a recent convert to Radical Golf, thanks to Pat, who acquired this volume for his birthday. He was a pretty good athlete and had played a lot of golf over the years. But today he leaves his woods at home, and it's just as well because Cypress Point is covered in bunkers.

Pat was always a Radical Golfer; she just didn't know it until she bought the book. She doesn't have much length, but she's straight, and deadly around the greens.

On the front nine there are no really short par 3s, but there are no long ones either. There's one very short par 4—number nine.

Cypress Point Hole 1
418-Yard Par 4

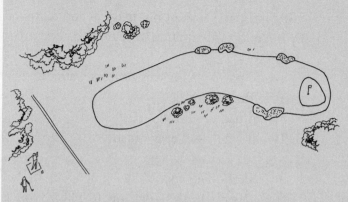

Will you have an overall philosophy for the first nine holes? _____

Which is: _____

What shot is going to be emphasized, if any? _____

_____

How many shots to the green? _____

And from where do you want to make your approach?

_____

(You may want to come back to this page and fill in the answers after you've studied the whole layout.)

Both Pat and Mike warm up easily on this long par 4, content to come into the green from the 100-yard area.

Both golfers miss their approaches to the side, then chip up near the hole. Mike and Pat lay 4 . Mike makes his putt; Pat misses hers. A 5 and a 6 on the scorecard.

Cypress Point Hole 2
551-Yard Par 5

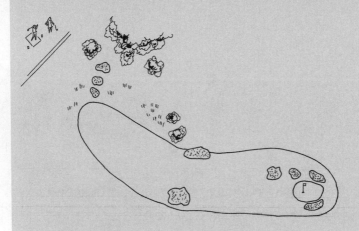

A longish par 5; how many shots tee to green? _____

What iron will you use off the tee? _____

From where do you want to make your approach to the
   green, keeping in mind the 50 yards of traps? _____

_____

*Both golfers decide to come into the hole from just beyond 50
yards. Mike uses 3 shots to cover 500 yards—180-yard drive,
160-yard second and third shots. Pat is still 100 yards away
after 3 shots. Both players hit the green and lay 4; both 2-putt
for 6s. No one's tearing up the course so far, and Pat has had
two 6s.*

Cypress Point Hole 3
161-Yard Par 3

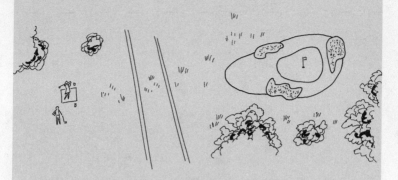

A shortish par 3. The big decision, depending on how you feel: Are you going to go for it?_____

Are you going to play one par 3 short and go for the next one? _____

Or both short?_____

If you hit the green, how much better chance do you have to get your 3 than if you played short and in front?_____

Is there a good landing area in front of the green?_____

Your final decision: _____

Are you going to emphasize the 160-yard shot on the entire round?_____

Mike hits the green and 2-putts. Pat is short in front, chips up, and makes the putt. A par 3 for both. A little better.

Cypress Point Hole 4
385-Yard Par 4

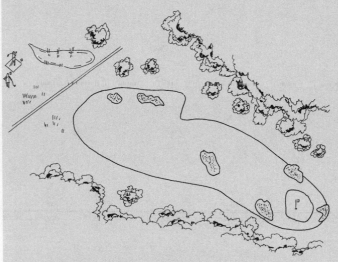

Have I noticed all the bunkers? _____

How am I going to play between them? _____

Will it just be easier to play really, really short? (This would mean using 2 shots to move the ball only 285 yards.) _____

Or am I going to hit a 2-iron and then a 3-iron off the fairway and go for the green? _____

How important to my score (shooting in the 70s) is it to reach this green in 2? _____

Both golfers play carefully because of the wind. Both hit the green from more than 100 yards out. Both 2-putt. That's two 5s on the scorecard. Pat is 5 over par; Mike is 4 over.

Cypress Point Hole 5

491-Yard Par 5

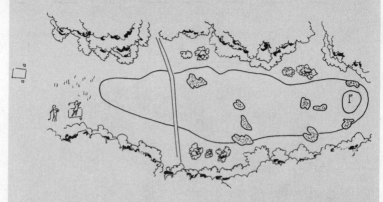

A short hole, but what about all these bunkers? Can I find a comfortable landing area between them?_____

_____

Can I reach this green in 3?_____

From where do I wish to approach the green?_____

Do I have a chance to birdie this hole if I hit a good approach?_____

A little better. Mike hits the green in 3 and rolls in the putt. Pat gets a par on this short 491-yard par 5.

Cypress Point Hole 6

522-Yard Par 5

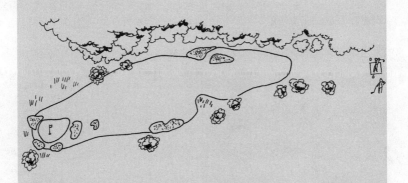

This is fun: the two par 5s in a row! Can I reach this par
5 comfortably with my iron in 3?_____
Could I birdie this hole with a lucky approach?_____
Or should I play conservatively in front?_____

*Pat comes into the green from 100 yards out on her fourth
shot and she 2-putts for a 6. Mike comes in from 150 yards
and 2-putts for a 5. Not bad.*

Cypress Point Hole 7

163-Yard Par 3

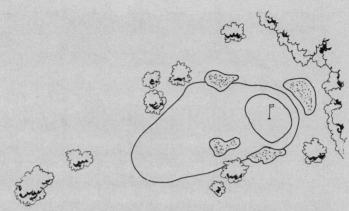

Here we are, another short par 3, more bunkers. Should
I play really short?_____

Or go for it?_____

What about the area in front of the green; what is it like?

_____

Should I wait and decide how I'm playing on the round?

_____

If I play short, how close am I going to be for my wedge?

_____

My wedge?_____

Or my 6-iron?_____

Or my 5-iron?_____

*On this second par 3, Pat chips up next to the hole for a par.
Mike rolls in a long putt for a birdie. Something to cheer about!*

Cypress Point Hole 8

355-Yard Par 4

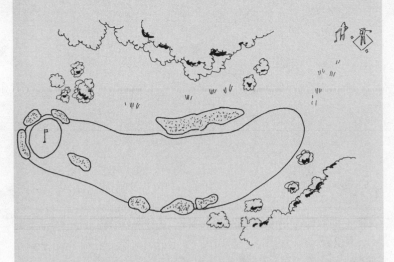

A dogleg. Well, it's a tough decision. You could smack a
2-iron and you might be in that 155- to 165-yard
range. Should you? _____
Or should you just play really short in front of the green
and chip on? _____

And let's see, you've got another short par 4 coming up,
only 291 yards.

*Pat uses 2 shots to cover 305 yards. She comes into the green
from 50 yards again and is right up next to the pin for a tap-
in. Her best hole. Mike plays a 2-iron off the tee. He goes for
the green on his second and rolls over. He chips up nicely for
his par.*

Cypress Point Hole 9
291-Yard Par 4

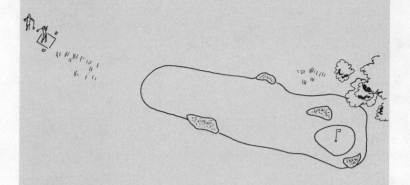

Gee, if you were to decide to play the short par 3s in 1 and play the long par 5 in 4 (that's tee to green) and you were to play those short par 4s in 2, you could go around this nine holes in 22 shots. Maybe even 21. Is it worth it? Maybe you should play the par 3s just for the area in front of the green. And use 4 shots on the par 5s. Play all of the par 4s short. You still wouldn't use very many shots tee to green. Maybe 25. If you putted well you could get around in the 30s.

On this short finishing hole, Pat is on the front edge in 2. Mike is on the green. Both Radical Golfers get 4s. So let's examine the scorecard for the front nine while in the cozy warmth of the clubhouse.

Mike	Pat
5	6
6	6
3	4
5	5
4	5
5	6
2	3
4	4
4	4
38	43	(On a par of 37)

Pretty darn good considering the start. But Radical Golf kept them away from the bunkers. They played within themselves and had some strong holes.

Let's look at the second nine holes. This is actually shorter, and a par 35.

Cypress Point Hole 10
491-Yard Par 5

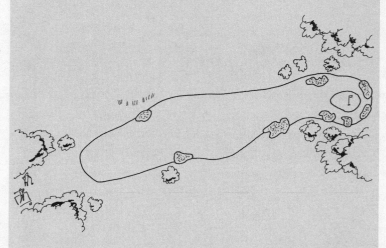

Well, you could decide to get off to an interesting shot by hitting that in 3. Or you could be very conservative and play up front and take 4.

Mike hits the short par 5 in 3; Pat plays her steady, short game down the middle and reaches the green in 4. Mike is still digesting his lunch and 3-putts for a 6. Pat rolls in her putt for a par.

Cypress Point Hole 11
434-Yard Par 4

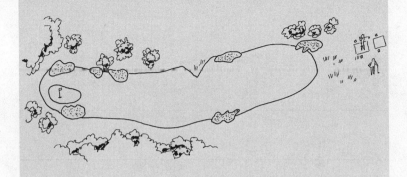

This hole is a more traditional, 434-yard par 4. It looks like a definite 3 shots into the green.

Mike misses his approach, takes 4 shots to reach the green, and 2-putts for a 6. Not the best start. Pat 1-putts for a 5.

Cypress Point Hole 12
409-Yard Par 4

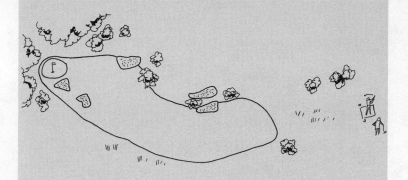

This is probably a solid 3 shots into the green. What do you think? _____

Mike lays up in front of the green in 2 shots, chips up, and makes his putt, finally, for a par. Pat takes 4 shots to reach the par 4 and 2-putts for a 6. Between the two of them they have a lot of 6s on the back nine.

Cypress Point Hole 13

362-Yard Par 4

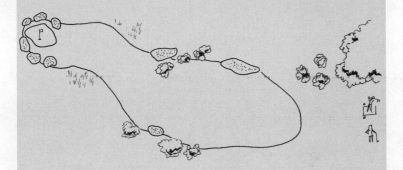

It's pretty short. It's got a green surrounded by bunkers.
   You could be tempted to try to make this green in 2.
   What's your inclination?_____
Maybe you should lay up and take the 3 shots. _____

_____

*Both Radical Golfers, neither playing well, take 3 shots to
reach the green and, fortunately, 1-putt for pars. At last!*

Cypress Point Hole 14

383-Yard Par 4

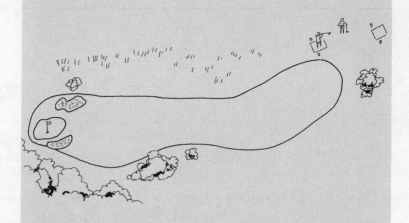

Also a dogleg. Same decision again, really: Should you
  lay up?_____

*Same deal. Both Radical Golfers need 3 shots and 2 putts for
bogeys. Will this mediocre play on the back nine ever end?
Yes, it will.*

Cypress Point Hole 15
130-Yard Par 3

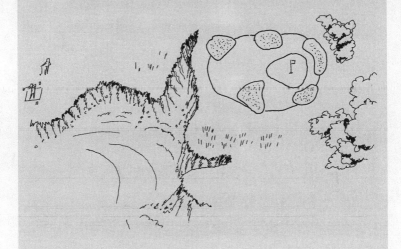

Very short. You'll want to go for this one in 1, probably.
Because the next 233-yard par 3 will definitely, definitely cause you to lay up. _____

*With four holes to play, Pat and Mike both hit the short par 3.
She sinks her putt for a birdie and he 2-putts for par. Pat goes
into an insane dance.*

Cypress Point Hole 16

233-Yard Par 3

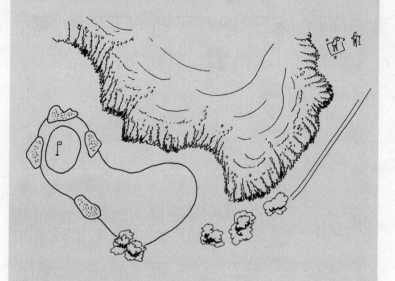

This is one of the most beautiful and most ominous holes anywhere.

It's followed by a 375-yard par 4.

On this scary long par 3, Mike gets a bogey and Pat a double bogey. Gee, they were feeling so good just one hole ago. It is a strange game.

Cypress Point Hole 17

375-Yard Par 4

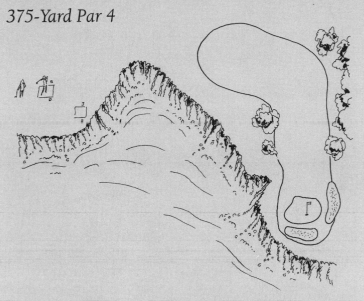

You can play this conservatively as well, even though it's short. You can lay up. What do you think? _____

_____

What will you decide? Because the next hole is the easy finishing hole. _____

The Radical Golfers, playing conservatively, both hit the par 4 in 3. Again, Pat 1-putts for par; Mike 2-putts for a bogey. This woman can putt!

Cypress Point Hole 18
342-Yard Par 4

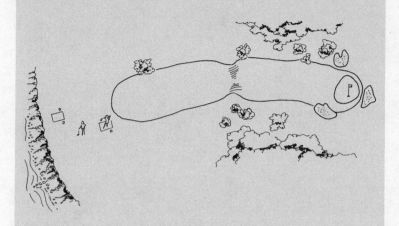

I think you can comfortably play this in two.

Well, what decisions will you make? I think you can play this back nine tee to green in 24 shots. You only have one par 5, which is unusual. And it's a par 35 overall.

An easy finishing hole after struggling on the back nine. Mike, in desperation, hits his 8-iron next to the pin for a birdie and a smile. Pat pitches up next to the pin in 3 and her 10-foot putt rims the cup and drops in the back door.

Mike	Pat
6	5
6	5
4	6
4	4
5	5
3	2
4	5
5	4
3	4
40	40

A couple of 40s! How perfect. Can this be true? It didn't feel like that good a round.

So Mike cards his 78 at Cypress and Pat matches his score on the back nine. Lay up and bomb the green. What a day!

Comments . . .

You know, I think this course indicates particularly well just how golf screams to be played with irons. Of course, I haven't seen your home course, but my instincts are that it does too. Most courses won't have the bunkers and hazards that one faces here. If you're serious about scoring, however, you may want to make, as a matter of habit, the kinds of decisions that we talked about here at Cypress Point.

Your Home Course

Now I'm just guessing, but I imagine you've had some pretty good rounds on your home course, and I'll bet there are some holes that you like and that you play very consistently. But there are probably certain holes that always give you trouble. And probably give you trouble in the same old ways. You're familiar with your course and chances are you've fallen into a pattern of playing it. So one of the first things we want to do and one of the goals of this book is to break that pattern.

The best thing you could do now is take some irons and play a couple or three sets of nine holes. Forget about the putts for now. Pay no attention to them at all. Just see how many shots—tee to green—it takes you to get around nine holes. Is it 25, or 30, or 24? Just get a feel for it. See how relaxed you can be. Whistle, if you want, while you work.

The Hazards, the Out-of-Bounds, the Lakes, the Ponds

That Always Pull Your Ball Like a Magnet

This is about perversity.

Most golf courses have an ominous out-of-bounds, or a lake, or a deep black hole of some kind that seems to have supernatural powers over your swing and the ball.

This power can have the effect of ruining a round emotionally—not to mention the score.

Other golf books don't attend to this problem. This one will.

Man, sad to say, is perverse. Woman too. If it's there, if you think about it, you will hit it in that direction, even if you set up purposefully so that you won't. This "perverse effect" is unnaturally strong.

I have done a certain trick a thousand times, and I'm sure it has profound ramifications beyond the golf game. You have the hiccups. Unrelenting hiccups. I take a wad of crumpled bills from my pocket. "Let's see," I say to you, "there's twenty dollars, forty dollars, a ten, four ones—there's fifty-four dollars here." Remember, you've been hiccuping non-stop. Involuntarily. I put the bills in your palm and say, "All right, give me just one more! You've been having no trouble so far, so what's one more? Give me one hiccup for fifty-four dollars."

No one can. I mean, *no one* can hiccup one more time.

The power of perversity. There's the lake. There's the fairway. You aim for the fairway—but hit it in the lake. Bingo!

So what's the answer? How can you keep hiccuping down the fairway? You've been hitting the fairway the whole time and then you think, "Don't let the ball go into the lake." Once that concept has entered your mind, you're cooked—there's no keeping the ball from swerving into the water.

The answer? Use the "perverse effect" to your advantage. Tempt the lake. Tempt the out-of-bounds that have always bamboozled you. Stare them in the face. Play right down the edge and tempt them to pull your ball in. They can't—and the spell is broken! Sometimes you just have to be cocky.

Three

Satisfactions

After what we've learned, we're ready for . . .
satisfactions.

Should a Man Ever Play Golf with a Woman?

My mother played field hockey in high school and college in the twenties—a pretty rough-and-tumble sport. I remember she had an injured leg—not so that you would notice, but it always seemed to me a badge of honor. I have a picture of her in her uniform with her team. She was a strong player. I played tennis with her when I was younger; she had been coached by Mercer Beasley in California and had great strokes. She played golf until she gave me her Patty Berg clubs. She was an avid professional football fan, rooting for the Cleveland Browns. For college basketball, she kept a scorecard.

My father told me recently that he can't remember her ever buying groceries or doing anything like that. Arrangements and tasks were taken care of, naturally, but it wasn't a topic of conversation or debate. Nor was my education. My mother made all of those decisions too, as well as the plans for my going to summer camp. In those days there were a lot of topics and areas that were just not up for negotiation. No hard feelings or anything.

Our home was certainly not a hotbed of political strife, but my mother did work for the League of Women Voters, and she was a friend of Adlai Stevenson's and supported him in his two campaigns for president. After college, my mother went on to graduate school and attained another degree. Her mother, a single woman who adopted her around 1917, was also a college graduate—before 1900.

My mom played bridge at the home of other women on certain afternoons, and she played bridge with my father on certain evenings in our home; she also liked to gamble in Las Vegas.

She and my father made the important decisions about the family business together, and he consulted with her before deciding to buy a beautiful Buick convertible in 1950.

The Bloomington Country Club had an all-male board of directors—probably still does. The grounds crew were all men and still are. The lifeguards were men *and* women. The swimming team was coed, naturally, and Bloomington was famous for its broad-shouldered girls. Back in the thirties, Bloomington had the first woman state senator in Illinois. When she visited a mental institution and said "I'm Senator Bohrer," they locked her up.

Bloomington had and still has two universities—one private, one public—and both are coed.

Women played golf at the country club on Wednesday afternoons. Men played on Thursday afternoons. The caddies played on Mondays. Many men, including the very best golfers, would often play with their wives on Sunday afternoons. And sometimes, of an evening after work, a father would play with his daughter.

There was, of course, a men's grill which was generally closed to women but which was open to everybody one night a week. My mother enjoyed dining there, but had no urge to go there on other days.

One of the great benefits of private clubs in general is that they allow members of all generations to meet on common ground—an opportunity that is not so readily offered by other institutions.

So to answer the question posed by the title of this section . . . Yes, definitely.

What Shots to Practice

Well, although it's probably obvious by now, here they are, in descending order.

The Wedge

1. The wedge from within 10 yards of the green is *the* most important. Make that ball run toward the pin and stop. I like the wedge as the club of choice because it eliminates the consternation of choosing between a number of clubs. I like the consistency of playing one club. I also like getting the ball in the air quickly and then letting it run. I think it's a better choice, also, for the amateur player moving from course to course, grass to grass, and green to green.
2. A little wedge from the 20- to 40-yard markers. Again, get that ball *up in the air, fairly high,* and stop it on the green. Just a nice consistent accelerating swing.
3. From the 80-yard marker, twice as far, it's a wonderful shot. And you should feel comfortable with this shot for the next 20 yards—between 80 and 100 yards.

The Mid-irons

Now we make a big change in clubs so that we are able to approach the green from the 140- to 165-yard markers. Seven-irons, 6-irons, 5-irons—whatever it takes to get the ball in the air to the green. An invaluable shot on par 3s and 5s and on the occasional short par 4s.

Putting

And finally, putting with your 2-iron. The short backswing and "pop" the ball. Consistent around the pin, consistent away from the pin.

That's it—wedges, 5s, 6s, 7s, and putting!

———

Several immediate benefits are going to accrue to you even before practice—just from the restraint and common good sense, the psychological benefits of not having to push for too much distance and then mis-hitting badly before you're even launched. There's going to be the relief and pride and confidence from playing your own game.

Golf is about playing within yourself.

Let's Review

1. One swing, one hand position.
2. Fewer clubs.
3. Better-designed clubs—more lofted.
4. Know what shot you will emphasize before going to the club.
5. Only practice specifically the shot that affects the score.
6. Your hands are in front of the ball. Your head is behind the ball. Always.
7. It's better to dress well and not take the game too seriously than it is to dress like a clown and take the game much too seriously.
8. It's not how far it is to the green, it's how far it is to your free throw area. The free throw is *everything*, your chosen spot to approach the green. If you follow this simple formula, you will score in the 70s: *On four holes of your choice, try to chip from within 10 yards. On three holes, perhaps including some par 3s, approach from 155 to 165 yards or less. Bomb the green from 40 yards.* This formula can put you in the mid-70s.
9. Don't complicate the short game with hundreds of different shots for different circumstances. Believe in a restricted short game of a few choices, just as you do with shots off the tee and fairway.
10. Success in golf is determined as much by what is *not* played as by what is played.

The Radical Golfer's Hot Round

And he can have this round! Perhaps *you* can have this round! And with only four or five clubs. How does he do it? How does he score well? The only way *anyone* can: by hitting approaches next to the pin or by rolling in some putts. Here's what it looks like.

Hole	Yards	Par		Score
1	347	4	2 shots, 2 putts	4
2	177	3	1 shot, chip close, 1 putt	3
3	430	4	3 shots, 2 putts	5 (bogey)
4	378	4	3 shots, 1 putt	4
5	512	5	3 shots, a hot approach, 1 putt	4 (birdie)
6	155	3	1 shot, 1 long putt	2 (birdie)
7	350	4	2 shots, 1 putt	3 (birdie)
8	323	4	2 shots, 2 putts	4
9	525	5	3 shots, 2 putts	5
		36		34

He was 21 shots tee to green and 13 putts.

On the back nine he's: 4, 5, 3, 3, 6, 4, 2, 4, 5. He took 22 shots tee to green and 14 putts for a 36 and an eighteen-hole round of 70.

The Industrialization of Golf

There is a trend, a disease really, that could be called "industrial golf." Maybe the disease can be curtailed if enough of us begin to go back to the game's intended form.

Golf is not played in carts today in Scotland, or Ireland, or England. The everyday practice there is to pull your clubs. Carts are not about convenience or speed, because, in fact, they are slower. A cart has to crisscross the course to find the two balls and deliver clubs to both players. The absolute worst comes when the cart must stay on a concrete path and you have to carry the clubs out to your ball. All of this and more comes under the "industrialization of golf" category and must be resisted if at all possible. It may not be. It's like encountering employees in bookstores who have never read a book and have no interest in books. There are courses today, regrettably, where true golf has never been played.

The Golf Course Has to Be Sacrosanct

When I was a little bit younger and just starting out in the film business, we needed a particularly exotic location for an important sequence in a film. After some debate we settled on Morocco, which if one was paying attention was referred to on maps at the time as the "Kingdom of Morocco." Now it in no way influenced my decision as a producer, of course, but the Kingdom of Morocco had built a very nice golf course in Tangier. Tangier is famous for other attractions—a university founded somewhere around 800 A.D., for instance—but the king had seen fit in his wisdom to provide a wonderful golf course as well.

As it happened, the king had a brother who was the head of one of the country's military branches, and our film company received "a request" by him to entertain some of our "girls."

When you are in a kingdom you are there at the pleasure of the king. As we were using his beaches and his mountains—his world—as our locations, it would not have been appropriate for us to have simply replied "Thanks, but no thanks"; it might have created a problem. I remember I was just making the turn from the ninth green to the tenth tee when the "request" was delivered to me. *Never allow a business message to be brought to the fairway.*

I realized that some of our "girls" would have to volunteer to join the king's brother and some of his officers for dinner. I discussed the issue with my caddie on the tenth fairway.

He felt it was not necessary to send *all* the young women to the officers, just some. I remember he felt I also needed a stronger club into the green.

No matter how enlightened a traveler one is, he unfortunately carries around certain prejudices, and I had a thought in the back of my mind that we might not get all our young women back by the appointed hour of filming the next morning—and maybe not at all, shocking as that is to admit.

I hit a firm 7-iron into a trap in front of the tenth green. I know now that I should have been cautious and played short. On the eleventh tee, I reconsidered the invitation. No, it was only for the "girls"—no mention of our actors, producers, or director.

Well, they certainly could not be faulted for that. No officers anywhere in the world would get that excited about entertaining blokes from England when there was the alternative possibility of foreign actresses, makeup and hair girls, wardrobe designers, continuity girls, secretaries, editorial assistants, and stunning-looking stand-ins.

I think I took a 7 on the eleventh hole. Maybe I should have just forgotten the round and gone back to the hotel.

My caddie suggested that I simply ask the young women to volunteer, and if none wanted to go, then pack up our bags and tons of equipment and head back to London. But that decision, of course, could be quite an expensive proposition for the production and for Twentieth Century-Fox.

I took an 8 on the twelfth.

Perhaps I should place a call to Dick Zanuck, the chairman of the studio, or get some guidance from his father Darryl in Paris. No, I thought, I should make the decision myself. I teed up the ball on the thirteenth. Much later, back at the hotel, I showed my scorecard to my colleagues. "Jesus, Mike, what happened on the back nine?"

Late at night a meeting was held among all concerned.

And as Allah is my witness, several girls went to dinner with the officers. The following days' filming went off without a hitch. It still remains one of my favorite scenes, played wonderfully by Donald Sutherland—much more wonderfully than I played the back nine.

We were back in London a few days before I realized that we were one young lady short—missing, AWOL, kidnapped, disappeared, never came out of the casbah, gone.

Several months later at the Cannes Film Festival, someone told us she had been seen shopping in Paris, covered in jewels.

THE ANIMAL KINGDOM

Forget what you have read in magazine pieces or heard—having animals on movie sets is not the professional experience that the public has been led to believe. Trained dogs, trained elephants, trained lions. Unh-unh. Animals are animals, whether in the wild or on a movie set or on a golf course. In a classic scene in movies, the western hero rides up to the farm and chickens scatter in the dust. How did the wrangler prepare the chickens for their roles? By holding several in each hand, swinging them wildly until they were dizzy and dazed, and then placing them in the yard before the camera rolled and the rider and the horse appeared. You don't train chickens!

In the movie *Kismet,* directed by Vincente Minnelli (he had many animals in his movies, for decorative purposes), the peacock spread his feathers on cue ("Hold my hand, I'm a stranger in paradise") because his feet were fastened with brads to the stage and he was goosed with a broom handle.

On a film with Beau Bridges and Melina Mercouri, directed by Norman Jewison, grown men cut the little suction cups off butterflies with tiny tweezers so that when Miss Mercouri opened a hatbox for her entrance and the special-effects crew blasted air, hundreds of butterflies flew out—being no longer able to hold on to the inside of the box.

These kinds of stories exist in the movie business, and there are just as many involving animals on the golf course. If you have good ones, send them to me. I myself have been chased down the fairway by a mother swan on more than one occasion. Don't hit your ball over by the baby cygnets! On Torrey Pines, a wonderful oceanside course outside of San Diego, I have encountered rattlesnakes.

Dogs have picked up my ball on the greens more than once.

My friend Henry was defecated on by birds several times in one round. There seemed to be no explanation.

Mosquitoes in Minnesota attacked regularly, and exclusively, our neighbor, a State Farm Insurance executive, and forced him and his family to move from Minnesota and return to the home office in Bloomington.

No-see-ums in the Bahamas make golfers streak for the clubhouse.

And we haven't even talked about the incidents on the courses of the African continent.

Where to Live or Spend Some Time If You Want to Play Some Golf

Well, New Zealand. First of all, the entire country—both islands—looks like one giant green golf course. Another big advantage to New Zealand is that it's not crowded; it's one of the least crowded places on earth. At least with people. It has a lot of sheep, maybe 50 million. What people there are, are charming. They will show up by the thousands to save a beached whale. They are real sportsmen, competing easily in the major world sporting events, even though they have no population. They have great roads, music, television and radio, farms and schools. And beautiful light. It's a magical place to play golf.

Carmel, Pebble Beach, the Carmel Valley, and the Monterey peninsula. Again, the whole area looks like the most dramatic golf course imaginable—and has, obviously, some of the most famous golf courses anywhere. As a tourist area, it has none of the usual negative trappings. It's like stepping back into the 1950s. It's oddly isolated—no big airports, really—which helps. It's foggy, which looks like golf. And golfers are respected there—there's no football or basketball franchises taking up space. It's just golf—and good food. Fish are held in high regard there.

Portugal is a terrific place to play golf. It feels like the thirties, maybe. They speak a language you are not expected to know. There are many fine hotels, it's not overcrowded, and there are many, many wonderful courses. People are polite, and they've been at it a long, long time. They have banks that financed Christopher Columbus's trip to the New World. It's a fine place to play golf. And not one of the first places you think of.

And who knows? Even Sweden might be good. After all, the country is producing major players now. But it seems so improbable, doesn't it?

The Radical Golfer Goes to the Hawaiian Islands

You want to play The Prince, a long, long course on the island of Kauai. It's the ultimate in "industrialized golf"—carts, concrete walks, starting times, all that bad stuff. But it's worth it in every way. Any course is puny after The Prince. The Prince is the longest, widest layout imaginable. It has all the delicacy of the water buffalo that graze nearby, but the best way to play this course is like you don't care, like you're just curious to see what a big, expensive, industrialized golf course looks like. Maybe shoot for the par 3s and play everything else real short. Stay out of trouble. Enjoy the sunshine. Maybe it will take you 27 or 28 shots tee to green. Who cares! A 42 or 43 could be a great score. And you don't even care. At the other end of this small island there is a Jack Nicklaus course—actually, two of them. These are big resort courses and complete "industrialized golf" operations. They practically shove you off the tee with a starting gun. But these courses *are* beautiful. You have to walk by lots of fake marble statues filled with sand just to get to the course. And this is after you had lunch next to a four-acre swimming pool right beside the ocean.

But it's perfect weather, so you might as well play. Just don't take it seriously. Put on any dumb costume you want—well, not too dumb—and get out there. And if you remember it's not really golf, you'll be okay.

There happens to be an absolutely delightful and beautiful course on this island called Kiahuna which you *will* want to play seriously. It was designed by Robert Trent Jones, Jr. It's a wonderfully landscaped and varied course full of surprises, and if you're lucky there will be a rainbow or two. It's the perfect course to walk and, chances are, not crowded.

Kauai also has one of the finest public courses in the country, along the ocean, and you can pull your own clubs. I should point out that, in my opinion, the greatest hamburger in the world—not even a contest—happens to be the one served on the island of Kauai at Duane's, alongside the highway on the way to The Prince. People have been known to take Duane's Onoburgers home on the plane and reheat them—which isn't as much fun, of course, as eating at Duane's under African tulip trees.

On the island of Oahu, forget the Oahu Country Club, even if you have an invitation. The day I played, golfers were getting bonked left and right by flying balls, and it just isn't worth it. It's a mountain course with a nice view down over the harbor, but more for goats who don't mind being hit by golf balls. There is a lovely public course on the island. It could well be the oldest golf course west of the Mississippi. (Missionaries loved to play golf.) And Oahu is famous for its military golf courses. If you're a member of the armed services, you will want to do anything that's necessary to be stationed in the Hawaiian Islands; golf is just one of the reasons.

There are many secret courses in the Hawaiian Islands, and one of them is on the island of Molokai. It, too, runs along the edge of the ocean. It's never crowded, for only six thousand people live on the island, and they are as gentle as can be. There's a nice conventional hotel next to the course. This peaceful, quiet, serene, magical setting offers one of the most ideal spots to play Radical Golf.

The island of Hawaii is just covered with golf courses, and the less said the better. Yes, some are quite dramatic: green fairways surrounded by dark lava. Mauna Kea is a perfect and magnificent resort course, but all that industrial stuff comes with it. There are local courses on the rainy side of the island that are challenging and fun. On Maui there are more golf courses spelled with more vowels than you can possibly imagine. The old-fashioned Maui Country Club is delightful.

Golf is taken seriously in the Hawaiian Islands, and that's a very nice thing. It's played by fanatic locals and crazy tourists, but it's all pretty wonderful. And it should be said that one can fly around these islands for a lifetime of golfing pleasure. The trade winds, the birds, the fauna, the rainbows, the climate (81 degrees in the winter, 86 in the summer)—it's not a bad life.

The Radical Golfer Goes to Scotland and Ireland

Royal Aberdeen, Prestwick, Gleneagles, Turnberry, St. Andrews, Royal Troon, Muirfield, Carnoustie, Royal Dornoch, Ballybunnion—just listen to the *sound* of these names. And if you *fish*, too, visiting Scotland is like dying and going to heaven. Scotland has the greatest selection of golf courses in the world. They can build all they want in Palm Springs or wherever, but this is it. Once you've played in Scotland you look at golf differently. Once you've played in Scotland, you may look at *everything* differently. Of course, this is where they invented woods, but that's all they had. Iron clubs came later.

These courses almost *demand* a Radical Golf philosophy. These are courses with long par 4s and 5s, and they are dotted with deep, deep bunkers that have their own names. You truly need a road map to play these courses, and nature plays the dominating role. There is the constant temptation for length on the long holes, but driving into a strong wind won't provide much distance, and the outrageous bunkers are everywhere. Low-flying iron shots that run mean a lot on these courses. Remember, you may not understand one word uttered by your caddie. But that's okay. He can still hand you the right club.

The Relationship Between Golf and the Free Enterprise System

There are not a lot of golf courses in China. There is one outside of Shanghai and undoubtedly more to come. There aren't a lot in the Soviet Union either, but maybe someday there will be; let's hope for the best. There's lots of golf courses in India. When they start building golf courses in your country or town, you can begin to think about investing in the area. This stuff is pretty simple. My hometown of Bloomington, Illinois, is booming. It has six golf courses and is still growing. The Japanese, who built an automobile plant there under the auspices of the great trading company Mitsubishi, bought their own country club. You may have missed the peak of the boom in Las Vegas and Hawaii, but amazingly enough, they are still building on the islands. Chicago constructed a golf course downtown on Lake Michigan. I'm not kidding.

Why do you think presidents of industry retire to Palm Springs? Presidents of our country too! It's not to write their memoirs.

Monaco, a principality so tiny it has no room for a golf course, has one anyway, and quite a spectacular one, too, above the town with a view of Mont Blanc. It seems that when you have golf courses you don't have a lot of *tanks,* a fact that should be borne in mind by many other troubled areas.

ALWAYS PLAY WITH A NEW BALL

My father and his older brother, Mac, lived on Page Boulevard in St. Louis. It was a nice wide street with small family houses. This was back in the early thirties, and often my father and Mac would join friends and drive over to Forest Park, a huge grassland filled with trees and lagoons and winding drives. Forest Park was built as the site of the St. Louis World's Fair.

There was a wonderful public golf course there. A casual affair—you signed up, waited a little while for your turn, and then you and your group teed off. In my father's group was a philosophy teacher named Edward Knight.

There was a unique par 3 with the tee on one side of a lagoon and the green across on the other. You walked around through the woods on one side and while you were walking, the foursome behind you teed off. And as my father tells it, the quiet stroll in the woods past the lagoon would often be interrupted by the sound of balls plopping into the pond. Every time my father's friends stood on the tee of this beautiful hole, Edward Knight—teacher of philosophy, Harvard graduate, a studious sort, not exactly one of the boys— would announce to those who reached into their bags and pulled out an old ball: "Gentlemen, you are setting yourselves up for defeat at the outset. Philosophically speaking, you are opening the door and announcing that you are going to hit the ball into the lagoon. It's very important that you always hit with a new ball."

Good advice then; good advice now.

Portrait of an Eighty-Year-Old Radical Golfer (My Dad)

My father plays golf as a lefty and tennis right-handed. Of course, one wants to learn just the opposite—to play tennis left-handed and golf right-handed—if you have a choice. He plays tennis regularly Mondays and Fridays, and he has a poker group that he's been a part of that meets Tuesday nights at the Ozark House; the game has only been going on for seventeen years. Some of the men in this group play golf. One is a marshal at the Masters Tournament in Augusta, Georgia, another plays every day—spring, summer, and fall—and one plays several times a week with his wife.

My father ordered a specially designed driving iron from an ad in the newspaper recently. Apparently it works, and it's designed to prevent hooks and slices. He obtained a second iron from the same company recently, this one designed to get you off the fairway and give you a little more length. So we're not the only ones who are thinking along these lines. These clubs work. He tried them out. He had a good drive, straight as can be, on a 380-yard par 4, and he hit his second shot off the fairway in front of the green and then chipped on.

He orders his clothes out of the Peterman catalogue from Kentucky, so he's organized as far as that stuff goes. Of course, in our family we have contests about who can wear good clothes the longest. I've got a great raincoat from 1956, but my dad has a camel's hair overcoat from 1950 that he wore just the other night.

But the important thing to reveal here is my dad's diet. Because that's the secret, and it's going to be passed on now to the public for the first time. My father begins his day with coffee and doughnuts—lots of doughnuts. Mary, his wife, might fix a little lunch for him around noon but, if not, he may have a Bloody Mary at a restaurant or the club, plus pasta. He likes soup, too. He's one of those people who ask, "What's the soup today?" If he's at one of the many country restaurants in the Illinois farm territory, he'll have a hearty meat-and-potatoes lunch, heavy on the gravy. My dad eats candy (chocolate), popcorn, potato chips, caramel corn, peanut brittle, salty nuts from a can, soft drinks, and of course martinis—good ones. He likes pie, especially in the country restaurants, and often fixes himself ice cream before going to bed, sometimes with a cut-up banana—for the potassium, of course.

My father reads *The New York Times*, the local newspaper, and the Chicago paper, but that activity is spread throughout the day. He tears out stuff for me to read or calls me. He came to visit me in Hawaii and I realized that his generation is more organized than those that followed. You see, if you live in Hawaii you have lots of visitors. And it's easy to make comparisons.

Visitors in their twenties don't get up real early and usually have lots of special medicines and prescriptions which they neglected to fill on the mainland, and this usually means trips to local pharmacies and lots of phone calls to doctors in New York. They are late to the golf course.

In their thirties, they are pretty manic and wound up from

their hectic careers in big cities, and often are obsessed with the idea of booking their return flights, which takes several hours of telephoning out of their first couple of days. Often they have trouble sleeping and are wandering around aimlessly at night through the coconut groves. They are nervous and distracted on the golf course.

In their forties they are relaxed. They seem to be at peace with the world but never really get out of the T-shirts and shorts that they slept in. And they never really get out of the coffee stage—most of them are still drinking cups at midnight. They get the yips in the pro shop.

In their fifties, visitors are physically active and read books. They've accepted things, good and bad. In their eighties—and I know some who are like this in their nineties—they still drive cars (although they worry about having to take that stupid test again), they love playing cards, they love their dinners, and they are thoughtful, fun, and wise. A lesson to us all!

Golf is one enterprise that never, ever bought into (to use that modern phrase), that never acceded to, ever, the cult of youth.

Founded in the 1300s, golf, like its more elderly practitioners, is wise. What a game!

Radical Golf Goes on Tour

Great Courses Where You Have to Know Someone
Pine Valley, New Jersey
Shinnecock Hills, Southampton, New York
Winged Foot, New York
Marion, Pennsylvania
Oakmont, Pennsylvania
Baltusrol, New Jersey
Medinah, Illinois
Hazeltine, Minnesota
Augusta National, Georgia
Olympic Club, California
Cypress Point, California

Great Courses Where You Don't Have to Know a Soul
Banff, Western Canada
Pebble Beach, California
Doral, Florida
Grand Cypress, Florida
Harbor Town, South Carolina
Pinehurst, North Carolina
Muirfield Village, Ohio

Wonderful Courses in Odd Spots
Pauma Valley, California
Rancho Santa Fe, California

Michael Laughlin

Desert Highlands, Arizona
Crans-sur-Sierre, Switzerland
Royal Calcutta, India
Wack Wack, Philippines
Scioto, Ohio
Tryall, Jamaica
Pevero, Italy
Valderrama, Spain
Royal Hong Kong
Lake Karrinyup, West Australia

Four

A Graduate Degree in Radical Golf

You've got the basic curriculum now for Radical Golf.

So it's time for a bit of the advanced course. Remember, the fun can be in the details. . . .

You Bought Your Woods, You Like Your Woods... When Can You Hit Them?

Well, the answer is not NEVER, but judiciously, ALMOST NEVER.

There are exceptions which prove the rule, but they are probably not the exceptions that you might think.

Maybe a 3-wood off the tee? It's not going to give you that much more distance and it's really not worth it. Maybe on a wide-open short par 4, but I really don't see the point. Maybe on a very long 465-yard par 4. Well, that hole is difficult—really difficult—to par anyway unless you're a professional; it takes more than one shot to turn it into a par 3.

What about those of us who like to hit 4- and 5-woods from the fairway? Well, now you're into a kind of golf that the Radical Golfer doesn't know much about. The professionals are not really hitting 5-woods, for obvious reasons, and the Radical Golfer would rather hit 7-irons, and 5-irons, and 3-irons.

But there are some players—older players, younger players, and some women players—who would need to hit a 4- or 5-wood *across water.* So that's the exception.

Oh, yes, there's one more exception. When every time you go out, you shoot a 76, a 77, or a 78 . . . then you can start thinking more elaborately about those oddly designed clubs, your woods!

Once Again, the Trouble with Woods

The trouble with the woods and the theory of distance is that it means you have to have the long game, the *whole long game* and everything that goes with it. And that really means that you have to have played this game regularly since childhood.

And it forces you into a position of going for long, dangerous approaches. If you are going to lay up, then there's no point in hitting the long wood in the first place.

I believe that woods are only a tradition and come from an era of match play, of gambling to win a hole, to birdie a hole, but that they don't make a whole lot of sense for the club golfer playing for score.

And furthermore, they can make for a very frustrating day.

The Absolute Most Important Shot

You're short of the green. You've played short of the green on purpose, or not, but the point is you're 20 or 30 yards short, and you want—you need—to chip up close to the pin.

The Radical Golfer is going to need to hit this shot many times a round. Certainly more often than the pros.

So, no uncertainty. Let's understand, once and for all, how to hit this shot.

You set up, in an open stance, facing left of the pin. Your hands are left of the pin, your shoulders are pointing left. The face of your SAND WEDGE is open. It's pointing directly at the pin.

Your knees are bent, the ball is back in the stance, the backswing is waist high, there's a little flex in the wrist.

Everything turns—well, shoulders and hips. Then the downswing . . . eyes on the ball . . . take a smudge of turf . . . follow through, staying down . . . club face directly at the flag.

Do You Need to Take Lessons?

No.

If you're scoring in the 90s, chances are you already have what it takes, and you don't need to take a lesson on your swing. As Harvey Penick said in his *Little Red Book*, ". . . you don't play swing, you play golf."

But you could take lessons on how to play out of the sand. Professionals are good at that.

Across the Sand to a Tight Pin

When you've laid up and have to play across a bunker to a green—a common situation for the Radical Golfer—open the face of the wedge. Choke down on the club. Take a steep backswing and lay the club underneath the ball. That's all there is to it. But then, of course, I like this shot, even if the bunker's not there.

Out of Sand to a Tight Pin

A very short shot from sand to a tight pin. Well, open up the face and set up so that your body is facing left of the pin. Then a slow backswing—nothing hurried—and out comes the world's softest shot.

In a Fairway Bunker

You find yourself in a fairway bunker. It's never great, but remember to take a firm stance—have the ball in the center—and just make sure that you make contact with the ball first. Do not scoop.

Fairway bunker—ball before sand.

The Knockdown

A knockdown—such a great shot to keep the ball low going into the green on a windy day. You need to choose more club than normal because it's a much shorter swimg—half to three-quarter swing. It's usually hit with a 7-iron through the wedges. Play the ball in the back of your stance—hands are

ahead, of course. Swing on a flatter plane, and you have a good low shot that will check up when it hits the green.

> **REMEMBER!**
> *Hold the club like a small bird—lightly. This is one of the most common mistakes. You only grip the club tightly when you find yourself in the rough or a hazard.*

A Bad Start

What about after starting a round with two horrible double bogeys—two 6s? Shouldn't I just hit my woods for distance and go for some birdies?

The Radical Golfer could have started his round with Tom Watson at Pebble Beach with two double bogeys and still finished with a 41. And if Tom had not sunk his approach or had missed a putt or two, he might have had a 39.

So no. You have to be true to your school and hope to bomb some pins and make some putts. Just keep playing to your "free throw" area. You'll be fine.

PRACTICE

Once you've incorporated the idea of Radical Golf, you will want to practice the shots that you'll be hitting the most.

And the question is, how much practice? You will want to practice putting, lag putting, and pitching. These are the touch shots. You will want to hit them with a lot of confidence.

Practice around the green can pay off that very day. Your muscles have a memory. Trust them; trust your unconscious.

With the other, longer shots, you'll have good days, and not so good ones. Days when you're hitting the sweet spot and days when you're not. But don't be worried, that's golf.

Twelve hours a week would be a lot of practice—almost like the pros. Five hours would be a lot. Three hours would be pretty good.

If you know you're playing for all the marbles—your father-in-law is visiting, or your old college roommate—then ten hours of practice the week before should put you in absolute clover.

I personally like to practice 7-irons and 5-irons. I like the feeling of routining off those shots. Hitting 5-irons and 4-irons off a tee is pretty good practice for the long par 3s.

But 7-irons, 5-irons, and a wedge . . . there's an awful lot of golf right there!

Breaking 80

It's no small thrill to break 80—a real sporting achievement, especially for those who are doing it for the first time. And for those who play golf regularly and have handicaps between 13 and 20, it is a supreme moment, one to be celebrated.

It's just a matter of rethinking one's approach to a game that usually produces so many mistakes and unproductive shots.

And you're fighting against a huge campaign from advertisements and prepackaged attitudes toward the game.

If you can rethink your approach and remain firm in your mind that you're not going to fall prey to the hype—and instead just advance the ball positively down the fairway—then you are going to improve by great leaps and your score will fall from one plateau to the next.

But you've got to practice around those greens with your chips; you've got to start believing you can chip a few in.

And on the green, with a simple short pop of the ball, the loft of your 2-iron will keep your hands in front of the ball—and this is what you need to improve your putting.

Simplify, simplify, simplify.

Write us when you break 80 and describe how you celebrated.

A Little Parable

You're planning a road trip. It's a ten-hour drive. You want to arrive before nightfall. It's important, for several reasons. . . .

It's your daughter's first concert. You don't see that well after dark. They don't seat latecomers until there's an appropriate break in the music. You are divorced from your child's mother, who will be there and have a lot to say if you walk in late. Your daughter needs to know you're there when she goes on. It's just very important that you be there on time.

Your vehicle is tip-top. The car has been checked over, it's been fueled up, you went to bed early, and you remembered your correct glasses.

You get off to a great start; no need to speed and get caught by a cop, with all that entails.

You're going along quite comfortably. It starts to sprinkle, but the windshield wipers work, so there's no problem.

There are more trucks than you anticipated. It starts raining a little harder. The passing trucks are throwing up water. You turn the radio off so that you can concentrate and not do something stupid.

At a truck stop, you are taken by surprise by a chance encounter with an old friend, an attractive ex-girlfriend. She looks great. She would like to have a cup of coffee; in fact, she would LOVE to have lunch. It's tempting, but you explain about your daughter's concert. She says, "Call me another day, when you're not so busy!"

You're on the road again, but there's an accident on the

highway. Traffic is backed up. You get out the map. Maybe you can go around, take another route, but it's unfamiliar territory. It's a definite gamble. Maybe it's time for a candy bar, or even a cigarette. Yeah, that feels better. Just be calm. See, the traffic is beginning to move again. As you pass the scene of the crash, there are lots of flashing red lights and the accident looks serious, between a big truck and a sports car. They're taking the drivers to the hospital. Makes you grateful not to be in their shoes.

Okay, now you're rolling again. You begin thinking about seeing your daughter.

And suddenly, out of nowhere—POWIE! RUMBLE, RUMBLE, RUMBLE!!

Oh, God, a flat tire!! The worst—and things were looking so good. You're doomed. Just as you'd suspected, everything is against you. You're not going to be on time after all. You might just as well admit that you'll be limping in late, as usual.

But now for the good news. It's not going to be like other times. You are a recent card-carrying member of the Radical Automobile Club, and you have your card with you. And more improbably, you have something you never had before on any of your previous road trips—a new cellular phone. The number to call is on the back of the card; you punch, and . . . by God, this stuff works! You won't have to try to change the tire yourself.

Back on the road, it's sunny weather. You're farther along at this point in your journey than you'd expected to be. The map steered you around a couple of treacherous areas. You remember both of them from the past—ugly, congested cities.

So it's time for a quick stop for food and a visit to the rest room. You begin to daydream of the early days with your daughter's mother. Days when you were young. Those were good days, weren't they?

And then the worst kind of luck—you've lost the car keys, can't find them anywhere. Everyone helps you look—in the parking lot, in the restaurant, in the rest room. It's so embarrassing.

But finally, someone finds them on top of the gasoline pump and your heart goes back to beating normally. You finish strong; the rest of the trip goes perfectly. You're early. Your daughter looks lovely and is thrilled to see you. Even your ex-wife has kind things to say. The concert is a triumph!

This is what a GOOD round of golf feels like, a 78!

Smoking on the Golf Course

Why not, if you're a smoker? Golfing is a long event, several hours, and nicotine helps your concentration. It makes for better connections in the brain. Nick Price smokes about six cigarettes per round.

A puff of smoke is useful for determining wind direction, better than throwing a tuft of grass in the air. I've known some who used a drop of ash as a ball mark, but I'm not recommending it.

One of the most outstanding NFL receivers of all time smoked in the tunnel of the stadium during games.

I'm not going to say anything about cigars. Except to say that a study at the University of Edinburgh in Scotland showed that cigar smokers live longer than anyone else. Think of it—George Burns . . . Winston Churchill.

And chocolate is good, too. Chocolate puts you in a good mood. Besides the energy it provides, it causes the body to produce the same substance that you have when you fall in love. And that must be a good thing.

Drinking on the Golf Course

Moderate drinking has been found to be healthy, good for you. Two to four drinks a day. Where one wants to have them is one's own affair. For most, it's with lunch and dinner . . . and after a round of golf.

I've heard of people in Hawaii who play golf after dark with phosphorescent balls. I'm pretty sure they were drinking.

The Crucial Chip

You just don't want to go through the process of hitting two or three perfectly struck shots to end up 40 feet from the hole and then flub the chip.

You have to have this shot, so here it is. . . .

Choose one club! (I like the sand wedge.) Don't make it too complicated with too many club choices and techniques.

One club—slightly open stance. The ball off the back foot, the same as in the pitch. You and your shoulders pointing a little left of the hole. But the club face pointing directly at the pin!

The club face must strike the ball with a descending blow. Don't try to scoop it.

Fade or Draw

Remember, these shots are not necessary for you to score a 78. But because they talk about them on TV all the time, it's good to be clear about what's going on. To fade the ball—that's from left to right—you must set up your body, with your shoulders on the line that you want to start the ball. And the club face must be pointing at the target. Further, you have to turn your hands left on the grip. That's it, swing away.

To draw the ball from right to left, you set up your body to the right, aim the club face at the target, and move your grip to the right.

I hate this stuff. I'm confused now.

Why couldn't fade mean draw and draw mean fade? Why couldn't high gear be low gear and low gear high? Why couldn't first-degree murder be the least awful and third-degree murder be the most awful? Are third-degree burns worse or better than first-degree burns? Is a gasoline truck flammable or inflammable?

Fade or draw . . . the heck with it. Just set up and hit the ball straight at the target.

The Radical Open

I'd like to see a tournament someday with professionals, and ladies from the LPGA, and good club players, amateurs. Everybody gets 8 clubs—no woods—and let's see who can play this game. Radical Golf. Could be interesting.

Golf as Mystery

Golf has a mystery and an elusiveness matched by almost no other sport. Maybe sailing, I don't know. Maybe fishing. But golf certainly has it—for both the professional and the amateur.

You can't dominate it. It responds to subtlety and luck; it doesn't respond well to a scientific approach.

Golf is more like a cat than a dog. I've heard it said that dogs are masculine and cats are feminine. Cats have a way of treating you like you're a professional can opener. Your dog would never do that. You have to accept the cat on his or her own terms. Golf is very much like that.

A psychiatrist once suggested to me that a golf course is like a woman's body. I have no idea what he meant . . . did he mean that first you "drive" to make an "approach," then you make a "pitch"? And that you try to stay out of the "trap"?

One thing I do know is that you can't overpower or dominate golf. You'll look like some fool chasing a cat down the street because it doesn't love or respect you.

Golf will reward discretion and respect. So keep it simple. Play short. Invest in a wedge. Remember Bobby Jones's putter, Calamity Jane, with the loft of a 2-iron. And remember how he dressed, too. Good luck.